Trauma Competency
A Clinician's Guide

Linda A. Curran
BCPC, LPC, CACD, CCDP-D

EAU CLAIRE, WISCONSIN

2010

Published by:
PESI, LLC
PO Box 1000
3839 White Avenue
Eau Claire, Wisconsin 54702
Printed in the United States of America
ISBN: 978-0-9820398-8-5

PESI, LLC strives to obtain knowledgeable authors and faculty for its publications and seminars. The clinical recommendations contained herein are the result of extensive author research and review. Obviously, any recommendations for patient care must be held up against individual circumstances at hand. To the best of our knowledge any recommendations included by the author or faculty reflect currently accepted practice. However, these recommendations cannot be considered universal and complete. The authors and publisher repudiate any responsibility for unfavorable effects that result from information, recommendations, undetected omissions or errors. Professionals using this publication should research other original sources of authority as well.

For information on this and other PESI manuals and
audio recordings, please call 800-844-8260 or
visit our website at www.pesi.com

DEDICATION

In loving memory of both
Elizabeth A. Curran and Gary S. Coladonato
I miss you, Mom.
Father Jerry asks that you say a prayer
". . . for a boy who couldn't run as fast as I could."

With much gratitude, to all of my clients for allowing me to
bear witness to your unparalleled courage and humanity.
As always, it is my privilege

To the icons in this field and my many mentors.
Special thanks to Dr. van der Kolk, Dr. Porges, Dr. Levine, Babette,
Rockstar, Bob, Mary Lou, Philip, David, Debbie, Jo and Carol.

To Jeff, for my corrective experience with adults.

And, finally, to David, Jamie and Jen for your love, patience,
support and encouragement. Without that, no book . . . no nothin'.

ABOUT THE AUTHOR

President of Integrative Trauma Treatment in Havertown, PA, Linda provides clients an integrative approach to trauma. As an individual and group psychotherapist, she works with simple and complex PTSD in adolescent and adult populations — including clients with co-occurring and eating disorders, sexual trauma, self-injury, and Axis II diagnoses.

Linda holds advanced degrees in both clinical psychology and public health. A Board-Certified, Licensed Professional Counselor; Certified Addiction Counselor Diplomate; Certified Co-Occurring Disorders Professional Diplomate; Certified Gestalt Therapist; Certified Hypnotherapist; and Level II-trained EMDR practitioner, Linda is a regional and international speaker on the treatment of trauma. She has developed, produced, and presents multi-media workshops on all aspects of psychological trauma. Linda continues to advocate for accessible, coherent, integrative treatment for all those affected by trauma.

TABLE OF CONTENTS

INTRODUCTION

Since nothing written on the subject of trauma would be complete without a mention of Abram Kardiner, here it is: After the Second World War, American psychiatrist, Kardiner re-introduced the concept of traumatic neurosis to psychoanalytic theory. Unlike his contemporaries, he recognized traumatic neurosis not as a conflictual illness, but as the result of a psychological defensive maneuver used in warding off trauma. He warned that the cost of such a maneuver might well be the destruction of the victim's adaptive capacity in the future.

Traumatic neurosis; a new name for an old condition. You may recognize it by its prior aliases. When it was a result of war, it was dubbed Shell Shock, Battle Fatigue and Operational Exhaustion. As a result of sexual assault or domestic violence, it was identified as Rape Trauma Syndrome and Battered Women Syndrome, respectively. As a result of childhood sexual abuse, it was labeled Hysteria. Describing the condition, trauma expert Peter Levine writes, ". . . it is the most avoided, ignored, belittled, denied, misunderstood, and untreated cause of human suffering." The DSM-IV-TR's most recent designation for this long-standing cause of human suffering is Post Traumatic Stress Disorder (PTSD). My colleagues and I call it, psychiatry's redheaded stepchild-the troubled one, who won't leave home.

Regarding psychiatry's erratic interest in trauma, Kardiner lamented, "these conditions [traumatic neurosis] are not subject to continuous study . . . but only to periodic efforts which cannot be categorized as very diligent." Since it is the collective that determines where its resources are directed, might it be that it is not only psychiatry — but society in general — that refuses to study trauma and its sequelae? In *Trauma and Recovery*, Herman writes, ". . . When the traumatic events are of human design, those who bear witness are caught in the conflict between victim and perpetrator. It is morally impossible to remain neutral in this conflict. The bystander is forced to take sides. It is very tempting to take the side of the perpetrator. All the perpetrator asks is that the bystander do *nothing* . . . the victim, on the contrary, asks the bystander to share the burden of pain. The victim demands action, engagement and remembering."

Quick recap of those options: 1) Deliberate, intentional sharing of another's pain, along with involuntary conscription into action, engagement, and remembering or 2) *nothing* at all.

Tough Call.

Introduction

Since the continuous study of interpersonal trauma and its sequelae would undoubtedly inform us of the magnitude of suffering borne by a multitude of victims, is it possible that the majority of us are (consciously or unconsciously) complicit with the perpetrator? It appears that way to psychiatrist, Roland Summit, who refers to our shameful collective response as nescience or "deliberate, beatific ignorance." In his admonition, he makes clear that we are not "naïvely innocent"; we are "willfully ignorant." This hardly makes sense. Why would we — human beings, herd animals, social creatures, living together cooperatively in a pro-social (at times, downright altruistic) communal setting — intentionally ignore interpersonal trauma and remain complicit with its perpetrator? The short answer is fear. (And, unfortunately, heaping shame atop of fear doesn't mobilize us; it further paralyzes us.) In all probability, we are unwilling to investigate trauma at any length — or in any depth — because we assume that we lack the capacity to bear the findings that study would generate. The most startling and devastating finding would undoubtedly be trauma's pervasiveness, i.e., the relative and absolute number of victims affected. These findings would necessarily remind us of the persistent threat to our own safety and the safety of those we love — bringing into awareness the blatant reminder of our own frailty, helplessness, vulnerability, and prior victimization. And, who needs that?

Societal nescience serves the same function as the psychological defensive maneuver commonly seen in severely abused children; mind blindness. Unable to bear the awareness of unremitting threat, child and society look away; neither wishes to see what evil lurks in the minds and hearts of men. Similarly, willful ignorance approximates the primitive defense, dissociation, which an individual employs during a traumatic event from which he cannot physically escape and/or defend himself. Mercifully, his biology affords him the opportunity to split off from reality. Once free from attending to the persistent threat, his body releases copious amounts of endogenous morphine, preparing for a blissful, painless death. Presented as the perfect defense for warding off trauma, dissociation is really but a forced choice among extremely limited options. Although this defensive maneuver is perfect, it's only perfect if the victim dies. Kardiner cautioned that if the victim lives, then (s)he forfeits his/her future adaptive capacity. Likewise, fearing that our resources to cope would be effectively overwhelmed, society has defaulted to the same defensive maneuver. Anesthetized and immobilized, we look away, denying and dissociating from reality.

But wait! What if we became aware that we were leveraging our future? What if the options only appear limited? What if the givens are erroneous and our assumptions wrong? What if fear has blocked our access to alternative, adaptive methods of coping? What if fear is just an emotion — one type of information alerting us to possible threat? What if we could see the danger, but not only the danger? What if we acknowledged the fear, but instead of shutting down our higher cortical areas and taking up permanent residence in the primitive areas of our brains, we continued to seek additional information — rational, creative, thoughtful information? What if we refused to learn helplessness? What if we looked inward and discovered that we have (or can develop) the internal resources to share trauma's burden of pain?

Plato said, "Wisdom is not only the foundation of all enlightened therapy, but the remedy for man's great sickness, ignorance (willful or otherwise). What if we were wise and didn't look away?"

10

With the recent advances in neuroscience and brain imaging, came discoveries and findings in the fields of human attachment, brain plasticity, and traumatology. These findings refute two of psychiatry's historical presumptions: 1) That trauma is essentially untreatable and only marginally controllable with medication and 2) The presupposition of a "talking cure." Knowledge gleaned has demonstrated that "intractable traumatic symptoms" aren't intractable; permanent "character/personality disorders" are neither characterological nor permanent; and for traumatic disorders, the "talking cure" isn't a cure. For trauma, it appears that talk therapy is, at best, inadequate, and at worst, harmful and re-traumatizing. But, fear not; we have learned something else. We have learned that in the context of authentic therapeutic alliances, mindful, somatic, body-oriented therapies transform — not only traumatic symptoms — but entire human beings.

In 1994, Ann Jennings wrote, "At this point in history, . . . multiple and divergent forces are confronting nescience with truth. Although these forces will continue to meet resistance, they appear to be forming a powerful movement. . . " It is against a backdrop of a new political administration touting hope, change, and personal responsibility that this movement should continue. At the end of the Second World War, Kardiner grieved the fact that "each investigator that undertakes to study [traumatic neuroses] considers it his sacred obligation to start from scratch and work at the problem, as if no one has ever done anything with it before." I wholeheartedly disagree. Currently the wealth of information available from various clinicians and researchers is not only plentiful, but also remarkably collaborative.

This book attempts to further synthesize current clinically-relevant theories with their applicability to the "therapy hour." It is a compilation of works from numerous skilled researchers and clinicians — reminded once again, that we need not start from scratch. Although every effort was made to credit the original source, when unknown or unavailable, gratitude and appreciation is extended to all who have looked inward and discovered that we have (or can develop) the internal resources to share trauma's burden of pain — all those who we were wise and didn't look away.

CLINICIAN'S CORNER: ESSENTIAL BRAIN STUFF
A REFRESHER: THE ANATOMY AND FUNCTION OF THE TRIUNE BRAIN

The term "triune brain," coined by neuroscientist Paul MacLean describes in evolutionary terms what he viewed as the three distinct but interconnected levels of the human brain: 1. The brainstem and cerebellum, (Reptilian Brain) 2. The limbic system (Mammalian Brain), and 3. The cerebral cortex (Neocortex).

1. **Brainstem and Cerebellum (Reptilian Brain):** The cerebellum orchestrates movement. The brainstem connects the spinal cord and the forebrain. It functions as an important relay station; every nerve impulse that passes between the brain and the spinal cord must pass through the brainstem to allow the body to function normally, i.e. it controls vital functions such as heartbeat, body temperature, and breathing.

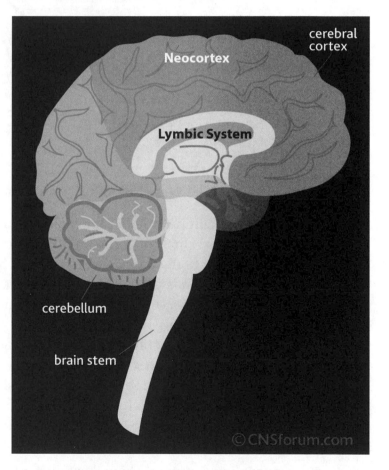

Figure 1 — Triune Brain

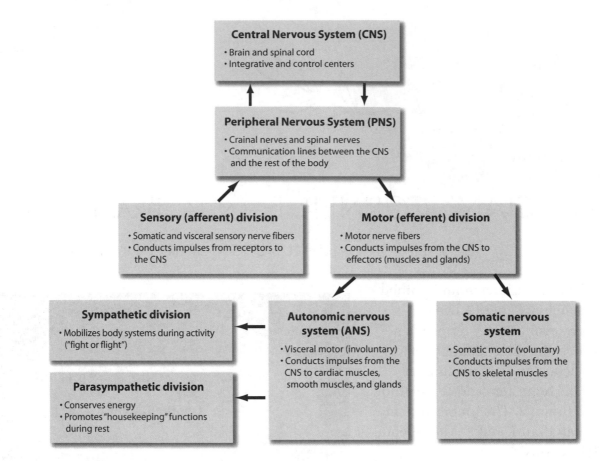

Figure 2 — The Nervous System

2. **The Limbic System ("The Old Mammalian Brain"):** A collective term referring to several brain parts, including the hippocampus and the amydala. The limbic system is tightly connected to the prefrontal cortex; and highly interconnected with the nucleus accumbens, the brain's pleasure center. It operates by influencing the endocrine system and the autonomic nervous system. It is the source of emotions and instincts (e.g. feeding, fighting, fleeing, and sexual behavior). The limbic structures are important in the regulation of visceral motor activity and emotional expression. Basically, the limbic system is the interface between animal drives and the constraints of society; between impulses and rational, practical decisions; and between crude emotions and "reasonable" behavior. The limbic system includes many structures in the cerebral cortex and sub-cortex of the brain. The following structures may be considered part of the limbic system:

a. **Amygdala:** an almond-shaped component of the ancient basal ganglia that is involved with aspects of emotion and memory formation — allowing for instantaneous, unthinking reaction in the face of a threat. As Joseph LeDoux says, "When it comes to detecting and responding to danger, the brain just hasn't changed much. In some ways we are emotional lizards." It is also involved in signaling the cortex of motivationally significant stimuli related, to reward including social functions including sex.

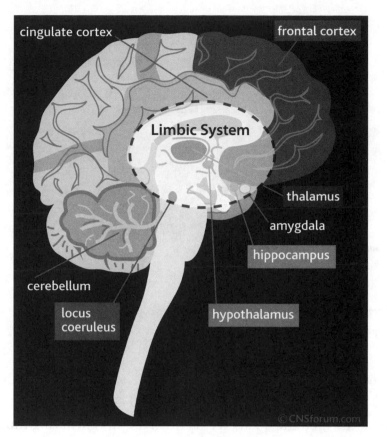

Figure 3 — Limbic Structures

b. **Hippocampus:** Required for the formation of long-term memories and implicated in maintenance of cognitive maps for navigation

c. **Parahippocampal Gyrus:** Plays a role in the formation of spatial memory

d. **Cingulate Gyrus:** Autonomic functions regulating heart rate, blood pressure, and cognitive and attentional processing

e. **Fornix:** carries signals from the hippocampus to the mammiliary bodies and septal nuclei

f. **Hypothalamus:** Regulates the autonomic nervous system via hormone production and release; affects and regulates blood pressure, heart rate, hunger, thirst, sexual arousal, and the sleep/wake cycle

g. **Thalamus:** The "relay station" to the cerebral cortex

3. **The Cerebral Cortex (Neocortex or "gray matter")** is found only in the brain of higher mammals. It is divided into sensory, motor and association areas. Sensory areas receive sensory input; motor areas control movement of muscles; and association areas are involved with more complex functions such as learning, decision-making, and complex movements such as writing.

a. The central sulcus divides the primary sensory and motor areas. Both the sensory cortex and the motor cortex have been mapped out according to what part of the

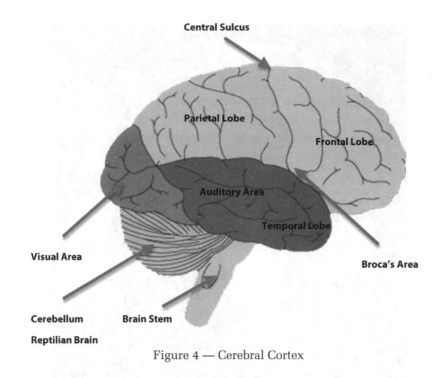

Figure 4 — Cerebral Cortex

body it controls. A larger portion of the cortex is involved with the lips, face, and fingers, which contain a greater number of sensory receptors.

b. Broca's area, the motor speech area, is involved in translating thoughts into speech. Impulses from this area control the muscles of the larynx, pharynx, and mouth that enable us to speak.

c. The visual area receives visual stimuli and the visual association area helps to interpret those stimuli. It is also involved with memory and recognition.

d. The auditory area receives auditory information. The auditory association area is where sound is interpreted as noise, music or speech.

Look familiar? Good.

Now a bit about fear and stress . . .

According to LeDoux (1994), the central nucleus of the amygdala is likely the control center for fear, receiving fear-related sensory information and transmitting fear-related motor instructions. He suggests that the amygdala receives input from three areas: the thalamus, cortex and the hippocampus.

- The thalamus and cortex convey information from the environment.
- The thalamus to amygdala pathway carries information rapidly to the amygdala. System One (Quick and Dirty)
- The thalamus to cortex to amygdala (Slow and Deliberate) pathway is more protracted-allowing time for the external stimuli to be *cognitively* appraised. System Two (Slow and Deliberate)

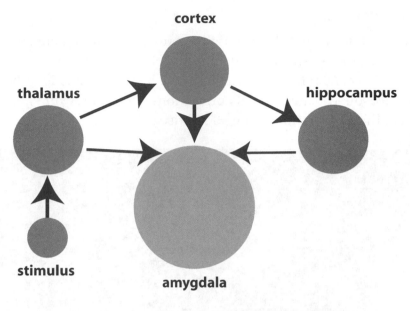

(From: LeDoux 1994)

Figure 5 — Amygdala Connections

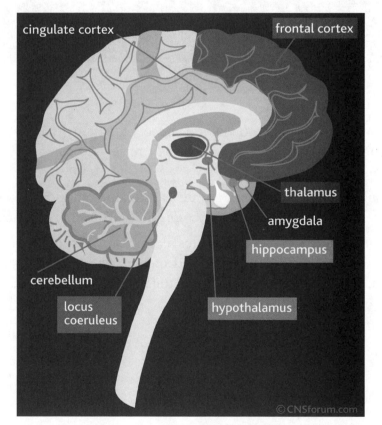

Figure 6 — Areas affected in PTSD

Remember the HPA Axis?

Here's the gist of it: it's a complex set of direct influences and feedback interactions among the hypothalamus, the pituitary gland, and the adrenal glands.

Here's the specifics: The release of CRH from the hypothalamus is influenced by stress and blood levels of Cortisol. The anatomical connections between the amygdala, hippocampus and hypothalamus facilitate activation of the HPA axis.

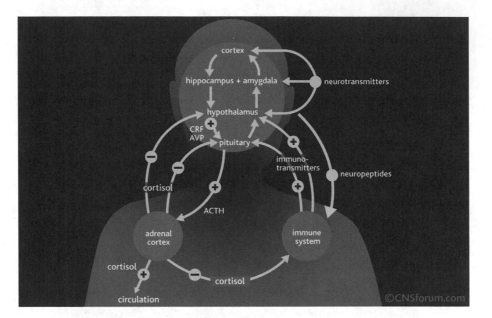

Figure 7 — The HPA Axis

1. Sensory information arriving at the lateral aspect of the amygdala is processed and conveyed to the central nucleus, which projects to several parts of the brain involved in responses to fear.

2. At the hypothalamus, fear-signaling impulses activate both the sympathetic nervous system (Figure 2) and the modulating systems of the HPA axis. (Figure 7)

3. Increased production of Cortisol* mediates alarm reactions to stress, facilitating an adaptive phase of a general adaptation syndrome in which alarm reactions, including the immune response are suppressed, allowing the body to attempt defensive reactions.

---

* Although Cortisol has the important function of modulating stress reactions, in excess it's quite damaging. Atrophy (and the subsequent shrinkage of) the hippocampus in humans and animals exposed to severe stress is believed to be caused by prolonged exposure to high concentrations of Cortisol and other glucocorticoids. The resultant reduction in hippocampal volume further reduces memory resources available to help a body formulate appropriate reactions to stress.

PUTTING IT ALL TOGETHER: THE STRESS RESPONSE

Scenario: You've decided to go for a walk. You aren't paying particular attention to direction and end up on a relatively unfamiliar road. From across the street you witness a violent mugging. You freeze momentarily, at which point the assailant begins running toward you. You don't think; you run. This is the stress response; it's automatic, thoughtless, and lifesaving.

It's only after your rapid retreat that it's possible for you to strategize a more reasoned escape plan/route. But, in the interim, your amygdala has sounded — and continues to sound the biological alarm — conveying signals to numerous parts of the cortex commanding them to pay attention to all relevant aspects of the situation (whether the man is following you, at what speed, etc.). At this point all energy is directed toward survival.

So, the hippocampus goes off-line, as there is no need for long-term potentiation of memory, if you're not going to survive to benefit from it. The amygdala continues to incite the arousal systems of the brain, harnessing and focusing complete attention on the threat, which in turn, signals and incites other relevant parts of the brain and body, including a cyclic re-excitation of the amygdala *until the threat is perceived to be gone.*

> "Plasticity is a double-edged sword that leads to both adaptation and vulnerability" (Shonkoff, 2000) "…It is the way the brain creates, strengthens and discards synapses and neuronal pathways in response to the environment. Chronic activation of certain parts of the brain involved in the fear response (such as the HPA axis) can "wear out" other parts of the brain such as the hippocampus (which is involved in memory and cognition) (Perry, 2000). Chronic activation of the neural pathways creates permanent "memories" which shape a child's perception and response to his environment.

All the while, the body continues its recon mission, sending alarm impulses back to the brain, reporting on the preparedness of the various organs and muscles. All of that information coalesces in the amygdala, which coordinates the fear reactions that keep you alive.

Just a little review. . .

There are two main pathways through the brain that are involved in the stress response or fear reaction:

1. Sensory input from the visual cortex hurries over the subcortical thalamic pathways to the amygdala. These thalamic pathways do not discriminate among stimuli (to insure that the message moves as quickly as possible), consequently, the information reaching the amygdala is *quick and dirty*: "DANGER!! DANGER!! DANGER!!"

   When the amygdala gets this message it immediately sends out signals to other regions of the brain-the anterior cingulate and the basal ganglia. Via the nervous system, the message of fear reaches the gut, heart, blood vessels, sweat glands, and salivary glands; the stomach tightens, the heart races, blood pressure increases; the hands and feet turn clammy, and the mouth goes dry. The skeletal muscles tense, and the smooth muscles increase activity, contracting the blood vessels and causing pallor. The pituitary gland sends its own signals to the adrenal gland (which will eventually send hormones coursing through the blood back to the brain to help deal with the stress). You *react!*

2. The second pathway takes the sensory input (in this case from the visual cortex) at a relatively leisurely pace over the evolutionarily newer, more precise, but considerably slower pathways to the cortex. This information is much more well-defined: "Big man, angry face, is that blood on his shirt?! That looks like a gun! And he's walking toward me. Get the hell outa here!" This message is far too time consuming to send, receive, and interpret. If you depended solely on your cortex to save you, you would have a very short life. When time is of the essence, this system fails, because it is just too deliberate and well, *too thoughtful.*

Once this information reaches your cortex, you can start to formulate your get-away plan. Via the thalamic pathways, the body and brain become primed for action. Now, what's needed is some cognitive input — a little thought, to refine your escape. The second pathway, after a short stopover at the cortex, continues back to the amygdala, where it meets up with the original thalamic pathway.

Once out of harm's way (i.e., the man is no longer in your vicinity), the emotional memory of fear and the cognitive memory of the would-be attacker become a learned emotional response that allows — and hopefully motivates — you to plan a little bit better for the next time. (Perhaps you decide to walk a different route, arm yourself, walk with a partner, or buy a treadmill.)

Because we have two systems — the quick and dirty one that keeps us alive and the slower, more deliberate one that allows us to plan a rational escape plan, we're able to effectively react to the danger (assuring our immediate survival of the encounter).

Once *the threat is perceived to be gone,* the hippocampus reengages, and begins the much slower process of transferring this stressful episodic memory to the store of general semantic knowledge. (Very little of what we have experienced is remembered as episodic memory. Instead, the brain extracts, abstracts and stores critically useful information from the sum total of our experiences (Schacter & Tulving, 1994; Squire, 1992; Stickgold, 1998b)) i.e. we take what's useful in this emotional memory (information to plot future courses of action) and leave behind the details, including the intense affect and somatic and visceral responses. This is what memory is for — to plan for the future; this is the normal learning process.

FYI: Formation of Semantic Memories

In the neocortex, memories are stored in dense highly overlapping neural networks. By a process called "interleaved replay", hippocampal memories are slowly and repetitively replayed from the hippocampal complex to the cortex where the memories are strengthened and eventually integrated and consolidated into the individual's general semantic knowledge (McClelland et al., 1995; Stickgold, 1998b). Thus, cortical memories, in contrast to hippocampal memories, which are sparse and quickly formed, are slowly formed and densely represented. Semantic memories are the extraction, abstraction and storage of critically useful information from the sum total of our experiences (Schacter & Tulving, 1994; Squire, 1992).

WELCOME TO "TRAUMA LAND: HOME OF SCARED BODIES AND LOST MINDS"

What happens when the threat is gone, but the person still perceives it to be present?

In PTSD the whole system (described above) breaks down (Ball et al., 1994; Lavie et al. 1979; Hefez, Metz, & Lavie, 1987; Claubman, Mikulincer, Porat, Wasserman, & Birger, 1990; Mellman et al., 1995), due to noradronergic and serotonergic surges. The information from the episodic memory does not get extracted, transferred or integrated into the cortex, so there is no weakening or elimination of the episodic memory. If the episode was a traumatic one, PTSD results. We see evidence of this in the constant, intrusive replay of hippocampal, episodic memories of the event(s), combined with the associated intense affect, but lacking the necessary neocortical input as to the semantic meanings of the traumatic event (Stickgold, R., 2002 *EMDR: A Putative Neurobiological Mechanism of Action*).

DIAGNOSIS: PTSD

"What's wrong with me?"

"Well, given your symptoms, I think you have PTSD; Post Traumatic Stress Disorder."

"Post Traumatic Stress Disorder? What are you talking about? Trauma? It doesn't make sense. What trauma did I have? I wasn't in a war, or survive a holocaust, or anything. I didn't even really get hurt."

This is a fairly typical client response to the diagnosis of this poorly understood disorder. It seems appropriate that this diagnosis — like any other serious medical diagnoses — would be initially met with denial (to temporarily protect the person from the reality of his/her own vulnerability). However, in order to effectively treat the condition, the diagnosis eventually needs to be accepted, and in order to accept the diagnosis, one needs to understand it.

To this end, I offer the following answers to the two most frequently asked questions: What is trauma? And, how bad does an event need to be to be considered traumatic?

According to, Dr. Peter Levine, "Trauma is a basic rupture — loss of connection to ourselves, our families, and the world. The loss, although enormous, is difficult to appreciate because it happens gradually. We adjust to these slight changes, sometimes without taking notice of them at all . . . although the source of tremendous distress and dysfunction, it (trauma) is not an ailment or a disease, but the by-product of an instinctively instigated, altered state of consciousness. We enter this altered state, let us call it "survival mode" when we perceive that our lives are being threatened. If we are overwhelmed by the threat and are unable to successfully defend ourselves, we can become stuck in survival mode. This highly aroused state is designed solely to enable short-term defensive actions; but left untreated over time, it begins to form the symptoms of trauma. These symptoms can invade every aspect of our lives." (Levine, 2006)

The most effective way I've found to have a client evaluate whether (s)he has been traumatized is to ask a simple question: when you remember the incident, is the memory exactly the same every time? With the same bodily sensations and emotions? If the answer is yes, then the memory is a traumatic one. By no means does one traumatic memory constitute a diagnosis of PTSD; it does, however, indicate that the traumatic event has been dysfunctionally stored; remains inadequately processed; and continues to cause distress.

A diagnosis of PTSD is different from most mental-health diagnoses in that its four major types of symptoms — re-experiencing, avoidance, numbing, and arousal — are all tied to an overwhelming experience. Which brings us to the answer to the second question: It's not what happened; it's how the event was experienced. What makes an event traumatic is the powerlessness and sense of overwhelm that accompanies it, i.e., an event is traumatic if the physical and psychological resources available at the time were insufficient for effective coping.

The symptoms that result from an overwhelming life experience may be stable and pervasive, or appear intermittently — sometimes surfacing years after the event. Usually, symptoms occur in clusters — growing increasingly complex over time (making it harder to trace back to the original incident and easier to deny trauma's impact). Although there are pervasive misconceptions about trauma, PTSD is neither rare nor unusual. But unlike seeking treatment for symptoms related to diabetes or glaucoma, seeking treatment for the symptoms of PTSD is somehow interpreted as a psychological weakness. Clients often tell me, "It wasn't really that bad; I should just get over it." To which I reply, "Then why haven't you?" Followed up with, "Don't you think that if you could get over it, you would do just that?" At that point, we begin the psychoeducation process.

DSM-IV-TR Criteria for Simple PTSD

(Reprinted with permission from The Diagnostic and Statistical Manual of Mental Disorders Text Revision, Fourth Edition, (Copyright 2000). American Psychiatric Association.)

A. The person has been exposed to a traumatic event in which both of the following were present:

- The person experienced, witnessed, or was confronted with an event or events that involved actual or threatened death or serious injury, or a threat to the physical integrity of self or others.
- The person's response involved intense fear, helplessness, or horror.

B. The traumatic event is persistently re-experienced in one (or more) of the following ways:

- Recurrent and intrusive, distressing recollections of the event, including images, thoughts, or perceptions
- Recurrent distressing dreams of the event
- Acting or feeling as if the traumatic event were recurring (includes a sense of reliving the experience, illusions, hallucinations, and dissociative flashback episodes, including those that occur on awakening or when intoxicated)
- Intense psychological distress at exposure to internal or external cues that symbolize or resemble an aspect of the traumatic event
- Physiological reactivity on exposure to internal or external cues that symbolize or resemble an aspect of the traumatic event

C. Persistent avoidance of stimuli associated with the trauma and numbing of general responsiveness (not present before the trauma), as indicated by three (or more) of the following:

- Efforts to avoid thoughts, feelings, or conversations associated with the trauma
- Efforts to avoid activities, places, or people that arouse recollections of the trauma
- Inability to recall an important aspect of the trauma
- Markedly diminished interest or participation in significant activities
- Feeling of detachment or estrangement from others
- Restricted range of affect (e.g., unable to have loving feelings)
- Sense of a foreshortened future (e.g., does not expect to have a career, marriage, children, or a normal life span)

D. Persistent symptoms of increased arousal (not present before the trauma), as indicated by two (or more) of the following:

- Difficulty falling or staying asleep
- Irritability or outbursts of anger
- Difficulty concentrating
- Hypervigilance
- Exaggerated startle response

E. Duration of the disturbance (symptoms in Criteria B, C, and D) is more than 1 month.

F. The disturbance causes clinically significant distress or impairment in social, occupational, or other important areas of functioning

ASSOCIATED FEATURES AND DISORDERS

- Painful guilt feelings about surviving when others did not survive or about the things they had to do to survive.
- Phobic avoidance of situations or activities that resemble or symbolize the original trauma may interfere with interpersonal relationships and lead to marital conflict, divorce, or loss of job.

The following associated constellation of symptoms may occur and are more commonly seen in association with an interpersonal stressor (e.g., childhood sexual or physical abuse, domestic battering, being taken hostage, incarceration as a prisoner of war or in a concentration camp, torture):

- Impaired complaints
- Feelings of ineffectiveness
- Shame
- Despair or hopelessness
- Feeling permanently damaged
- A loss of previously sustained beliefs
- Hostility
- Social withdrawal
- Feeling constantly threatened
- Impaired relationships with others
- A change from the individual's previous personality characteristics

DSM–IV–TR Criteria for Complex PTSD
A New Concept

Even the diagnosis of "Post-Traumatic Stress Disorder," as it is presently defined, does not fit accurately enough. The existing diagnostic criteria for this disorder are derived mainly from survivors of circumscribed traumatic events. They are based on the prototypes of combat, disaster, and rape. In survivors of prolonged, repeated trauma, the symptom picture is often far more complex. Survivors of prolonged abuse develop characteristic personality changes, including deformations of relatedness and identity. Survivors of abuse in childhood develop similar problems with relationships and identity; in addition, they are particularly vulnerable to repeated harm, both self-inflicted and at the hands of others. The current formulation of post-traumatic stress disorder fails to capture either the protean symptomatic manifestations of prolonged, repeated trauma or the profound deformations of personality that occur in captivity. The syndrome that follows upon prolonged repeated trauma needs its own name. I propose to call it "complex post-traumatic stress disorder." The responses to trauma are best understood as a spectrum of conditions rather than as a single disorder. They range from a brief stress reaction that gets better by itself and never qualifies for a diagnosis, to classic or simple post-traumatic stress disorder, to the complex syndrome of prolonged, repeated trauma. As the concept of a complex traumatic syndrome has gained wider recognition, it has been given several additional names. The working group for the diagnostic manual of the American Psychiatric Association has chosen the designation "disorder of extreme stress not otherwise specified". . . Naming the syndrome of complex post-traumatic stress disorder represents an essential step toward granting those who have endured prolonged exploitation a measure of the recognition they deserve. It is an attempt to find a language that is at once faithful to the traditions of accurate psychological observation and to the moral demands of traumatized people. It is an attempt to learn from survivors, who understand, more profoundly than any investigator, the effects of captivity (1992, 1997).

> Excerpted from the seminal work of Judith Herman, *Trauma and Recovery*

About her participation in the PTSD Working Group for DSM-IV, Herman writes,

The data seemed promising: my co-investigators and I found that somatization, dissociation, and affect dysregulation — three cardinal symptoms of complex PTSD — were found particularly in survivors of childhood abuse, less commonly in those abused in adolescence or adulthood, and rarely in people who had endured a single acute trauma that was not of human design. Moreover, these three groups of symptoms were highly intercorrelated (van der Kolk et al., 1996).

> Herman, J.L. 2009 in *Treating Complex Traumatic Stress Disorders*
> *An Evidence-Based Guide,* Edited by Christine A. Courtois and
> Julian D. Ford (pp. xiii-xvii). NY, NY:Guilford

van der Kolk summarized,

Abused and neglected children, and many adults with histories of abuse and neglect, tend to suffer from 1) a lack of a predictable sense of self, with a poor sense of separateness, and a disturbed body image, 2) poorly modulated affect and impulse control, including aggression against self and others, and 3) uncertainty about the reliability and predictability of others. This accounts for the distrust, suspiciousness, problems with intimacy, and social isolation seen in many individuals with these histories. Cole & Putnam (1992) have proposed that people's core sense of self is, to a substantial degree, defined by their capacity to regulate internal states and by how well they can predict and regulate their responses to stress (van der Kolk, 2001).

We thought this demonstration of the prevalence and internal consistency of the diagnosis would constitute a strong argument for its inclusion in the DSM, and the PTSD Working Group agreed. Unfortunately, we were overruled at higher levels. The argument against inclusion of a separate diagnosis, as I understood it, went something like this: "We can't include complex PTSD as part of the trauma spectrum because it does not fit neatly under the category of anxiety disorders. It might fit equally well under dissociative disorders, or somatization disorders, or even personality disorders." This was, of course, exactly the point.

And exactly why complex PTSD needed its own designation, but was unfortunately relegated to the "Associated Features" under the diagnosis of PTSD. She goes on to elucidate the etiology of complex trauma,

The "characterological" features of complex PTSD start to make sense if one imagines how a child might develop within a relational matrix in which the strong do as they please, the weak submit, caretakers seem willfully blind, and there is no one to turn to for protection. (Herman, 2009)

PROPOSED CRITERIA FOR COMPLEX PTSD

1. A History of subjection to totalitarian control over a prolonged period (months to years).

2. Alterations in Affect Regulation, including:
   - Persistent dysphoria
   - Chronic suicidal preoccupation
   - Self-injury
   - Explosive or extremely inhibited anger (may alternate)
   - Compulsive or extremely inhibited sexuality (may alternate)

3. Alterations in Consciousness, including:
   - Amnesia or hypermnesia for traumatic events
   - Transient dissociative episodes
   - Depersonalization/derealization
   - Reliving experiences, either in the form of intrusive post-traumatic stress disorder symptoms or in the form of ruminative preoccupation

4. Alterations in Self-perception, including:
   - Sense of helplessness or paralysis of initiative
   - Shame, guilt, and self-blame
   - Sense of defilement or stigma
   - Sense of complete difference from others (may include sense of specialness, utter aloneness, belief no other person can understand, or nonhuman identity)

5. Alterations in Perception of Perpetrator, including:
   - Preoccupation with relationship with perpetrator (includes preoccupation with revenge)
   - Unrealistic attribution of total power to perpetrator (caution: victim's assessment of power realities may be more realistic than clinician's)
   - Idealization or paradoxical gratitude
   - Sense of special or supernatural relationship
   - Acceptance of belief system or rationalizations of perpetrator

6. Alterations in Relations with Others, including:
   - Isolation and withdrawal
   - Disruption in intimate relationships
   - Repeated search for rescuer (may alternate with isolation and withdrawal)
   - Persistent distrust
   - Repeated failures of self-protection

7. Alterations in systems of Meaning
   - Loss of sustaining faith
   - Sense of hopelessness and despair

(Herman, 2002)

It would be hard to overlook the remarkable parallel between the symptom clusters of Borderline Personality Disorder and Complex PTSD. Both disorders include affect dysregulation, disorders of self, suicidality, dissociation, substance abuse, self harm, and relational difficulties (APA, 1994; Driessen, et al., 2002; Gunderson & Sabo, 1993; McLean, & Gallop, 2003; Yen, et al., 2002), and both involve very similar psychobiological problems (Driessen et al., 2002).

DSM-IV-TR Criteria for Borderline Personality Disorder

(Reprinted with permission from The Diagnostic and Statistical Manual of Mental Disorders Text Revision, Fourth Edition, (Copyright 2000). American Psychiatric Association.)

1. Frantic efforts to avoid real or imagined abandonment.

    a. Note: Do not include suicidal or self-mutilating behavior covered in Criterion 5.

2. A pattern of unstable and intense interpersonal relationships characterized by alternating between extremes of idealization and devaluation.

3. Identity disturbance: markedly and persistently unstable self-image or sense of self.

4. Impulsivity in at least two areas that are potentially self-damaging (e.g., spending, sex, substance abuse, reckless driving, binge eating). Note: Do not include suicidal or self-mutilating behavior covered in Criterion 5.

5. Recurrent suicidal behavior, gestures, or threats, or self-mutilating behavior

6. Affective instability due to a marked reactivity of mood (e.g., intense episodic dysphoria, irritability, or anxiety usually lasting a few hours and only rarely more than a few days).

7. Chronic feelings of emptiness

8. Inappropriate, intense anger or difficulty controlling anger (e.g., frequent displays of temper, constant anger, recurrent physical fights)

9. Transient, stress-related paranoid ideation or severe dissociative symptoms

The essential feature of Borderline Personality Disorder is a pervasive pattern of instability of interpersonal relationships, self-image, and affects, and marked impulsivity that begins by early adulthood and is present in a variety of contexts.

Individuals with Borderline Personality Disorder make frantic efforts to avoid real or imagined abandonment (Criterion 1). The perception of impending separation or rejection, or the loss of external structure, can lead to profound changes in self-image, affect, cognition, and behavior. These individuals are very sensitive to environmental circumstances. They experience intense abandonment fears and inappropriate anger, even when faced with a realistic time-limited separation or when there are unavoidable changes in plans. They may believe that this "abandonment" implies they are "bad." These abandonment fears are related to an intolerance of being alone and a need to have other people with them. Their frantic efforts to avoid abandonment may include impulsive actions such as self-mutilating or suicidal behaviors, which are described separately in Criterion 5.

To a great extent, the existing knowledge of Complex PTSD comes from a reframing of the diagnosis of Borderline Personality Disorder (Herman, et al., 1989; Zanarini, et al., 1997). Until relatively recently, the research on the treatment of BPD, conducted by Marsha Linehan, had either not recognized or disregarded the disorder's traumatic origins, but instead, focused on functional stabilization. This author contests that Linehan ignored BPD's traumatic origins, as trauma is explicitly addressed in Stage Two of DBT. However, realistically and pragmatically, was/is there a reason to address traumatic origins in the preliminary stage of therapy with this population, consisting of unstable, decompensating — if not actively suicidal — clients? Probably not.

In addition, through a researcher's lens, it would make little sense to target trauma as the primary focus of treatment when the research seemed to indicate that *not all clients who fit criteria for BPD reported a history of childhood abuse or neglect.* (This author takes a different perspective with regard to what is considered traumatic. For clarification, the reader is directed to the chapter on intergenerational trauma and disorganized/disoriented attachment trauma. See Hess, Main, Abrams, and Rifkin in Solomon & Siegel's, *Healing Trauma*, 2003).

Although Dr. Linehan, the clinician, humbly admits that her various attempts to employ straight behavioral therapy with this population resulted in abject failure, her thwarted attempts became the impetus for the development of an alternative approach; Dialectical Behavior Therapy (DBT). Linehan's dialectical approach has yielded great success with this very difficult population. DBT facilitates improvement in affect regulation, thereby decreasing the need to self-medicate via rather costly coping methods, facilitates the development of an observing ego, enhances effective communication, improves self-efficacy, and strengthens ego. As we are, in essence, treating similar developmental deficits, it should come as no surprise that these skills would transfer, becoming an excellent foundation for the treatment of Complex PTSD.

Without belaboring the point, it should be somewhat evident by now that there is nothing inherently wrong with these clients; they've made brilliant and creative adaptations to dysfunctional environments in the name of survival. Biologically, emotionally, and cognitively, they are effectively "hardwired" to endure their originally abusive and/or negligent environment; the problem is that their environment has changed.

Even though therapy will not resolve all of the problems that are associated with early traumatic stress, they do offer hope. Clients should be informed that a choice is required, and there are limited options: the first is familiar, requires little effort, but offers little optimism regarding significant improvement. The second feels alien, impossibly difficult, somewhat overwhelming, requires an enormous amount of effort, but does offer hope of a better life. Concisely, the options are: 1) Find (or continue to inhabit) an environment that replicates the original one — no brain changes are necessary or 2) Accept the unfortunate truth of their traumatic past and its resultant brain changes, and begin to rewire his/her brain for the present.

Theoretically, its simplicity is no less than staggering; clinically, its complexity is no less than staggering.

STAGES OF THERAPY

Stages of Therapy: Overview

Although the prevailing wisdom divides therapy into three distinct stages: *Stabilization, Working Through of Trauma,* and *Reintegration/Reconnection with Society,* this book's focus is mainly on the first two — stabilization and working through of trauma. These two stages, although not rigidly divided, are separate in their goals (and concretely labeled as such), whereas stage three's goals seem borne out of (and recognized in) both stage one and stage two of therapy.

Finally, some folks may disagree, diagnosis and assessment are in and of themselves therapeutic interventions, and, as such, will be included in stage one.

Stage One, Stabilization: Overview

As per convention, we will define stabilization as relative freedom from crises or significant emotional, behavioral, and/or relational turmoil. Ultimately, the process of therapeutic stabilization involves preparing a client to sufficiently think and feel simultaneously, so that (s)he may proactively exert agency in the task of making safe, effective choices in service of a coherently organized self. In order to accomplish this ambitious feat, the treatment process — within a safe, secure therapeutic relationship — should be geared toward the development of self-awareness and emotional intelligence and the repair of faulty information processing skills.

- **Therapeutic Relationship:** *Safety,* rapport, *Safety,* trust and *Safety* are of such critical importance that it can't be overstated. Establishing a therapeutic alliance is hardly an initial step to be completed; rather it must be diligently attended to, session in and session out.

  Extolling the wonders of EMDR, van der Kolk once diminished the necessity of the therapeutic relationship, stating that clinicians "should be more like plumbers than priests"; he has since revised his position. He, along with most trauma experts, is now acutely aware of the need for preliminary attachment work prior to trauma reprocessing with truly traumatized individuals.

  > After intense efforts to ward off reliving the trauma, therapists cannot expect that the resistances to remember will suddenly melt away under their empathic efforts. The trauma can only be worked through when a secure bond is established with another person; this then can be utilized to hold the psyche together when the threat of physical disintegration is re-experienced. (van der Kolk, van der Hart, Burbridge, 1995)

The absence of an authentic therapeutic relationship not only interferes with, but, in fact, precludes healing, as clients do not *grow out of* early attachment schemas. Herman looks to Bowlby's internal working model (1973) and asks the clinician to ponder the question,

What kind of self, other, and relationship would be likely to develop under such (traumatic stress in childhood) circumstances?. . . One begins to understand the survivor's malignant self-loathing, the deep mistrust of others, and the template for relational reenactments that the survivor carries into adult life. Forming a therapeutic alliance becomes somewhat easier if the clinician understands at the outset why the patient might be unable to imagine a relationship that is genuinely caring, freely chosen, fair to both parties, mutually attuned, and mutually rewarding. It becomes the therapist's task, then, to model, explain, and engage the patient in such a relationship, knowing that initially the patient will perceive this as another likely setup for betrayal. (Herman, 2009)

- **Clinical Assessment:** "Distinguishing between complex trauma and other forms of psychological trauma, and between complex traumatic stress disorders and post-traumatic stress disorder (PTSD) as currently defined in the text revision of the fourth edition of the *Diagnostic and Statistical Manual of Mental Disorders* (DSM-IV-TR; American Psychiatric Association, 2000), makes a substantial difference in clinical assessment and treatment." (Ford & Courtois, 2009). Clinical assessment of clients with complex trauma histories should include: a detailed assessment of current functioning and current stressors; a detailed history of traumatic stress; comprehensive assessment of childhood abuse/neglect and subsequent attachment issues (insecure disoriented/disorganized attachment pattern is commonly associated with pervasive abuse/neglect in childhood); a detailed assessment of affective dysregulation; somatic and visceral dysregulation; cognitive dysfunction; relational impairment, along with core issues, such as distorted views of self and others, and limited self-regulatory and interpersonal skills. (*See* Assessment Instruments following this section)

- **Diagnosis/Development of Crisis Plan:** After assessing the client's current condition, diagnose if/when appropriate, and co-create a plan for treatment. If the client is in current danger from internal or external threats, i.e., physical danger at the hands of self or other, that must be given priority. (See next section)

- **Symptom Recognition and Management**

  A. **Symptom Recognition:** Although the costly behaviors are recognized and explicitly acknowledged as the client's best attempts at adaptation, the clinician will begin to facilitate connections between the client's internal states of distress and his/her current destructive behaviors including:

  1. Violence Against Others

  2. Self Inflicted Violence

  3. Addictive/Compulsive Behaviors:

     a. Sex

     b. Eating

     c. Gambling

    d. Drug and Alcohol

B. Symptom Management:

    1. Medication Assessment and Management

    2. DBT/CBT and skills training:

        a. Emotion Regulation

        b. Distress Tolerance

        c. Interpersonal Communication

        d. Mindfulness

    3. Mentalization Training

    4. Meridian-based interventions for physiological arousal reduction: (acupressure points, containment poses, etc.), EFT, a.k.a. tapping, etc.

    5. Guided Visualization for self-soothing and imaginal internal resourcing

- **Identify and Incorporate Client Strengths and Resources**

    1. Narrative Therapy offers clients opportunity to "thicken the story." In order for clients to be freed from the influence of traumatic stories, it is not enough to simply re-author an alternative one. Narrative therapy is interested in finding ways to "richly describe" the alternative story. Rich description involves the articulation in fine detail of the story lines of a person's life. Like in all richly described stories, to write one, the client needs to reflect on the history, motives, strengths and weaknesses of not only his/her own character, but on all of the principal characters in his/her life. (For further information, see reference on page 216)

    2. According to van der Kolk,

PTSD symptoms should not be treated until the available internal and external resources have been identified and are in place: skills, hobbies, activities that calm the patient down, give satisfaction and a sense of competence. For most people feelings of interpersonal safety are essential to provide the sense of inner calm to make a distinction between current situations and the roots of current distress in the past. Fear needs to be tamed in order for people to be able to think clearly and be conscious of what they currently need. For this, it is necessary to have a body with predictable and controllable reactions. (van der Kolk, 2001)

Stage Two, Working Through Trauma: Overview

. . . Treatment modalities for complex traumatic stress disorders are most effective if the clinician focuses on using them as a vehicle for enhancing self-reflective processing of emotion and information (i.e., bodily sensations, perceptions, thoughts, intentions, plans, appraisals) rather than simply limiting the focus to overcoming avoidance of traumatic memories. With enhanced emotion and information processing comes a corresponding increase in the capacity to choose not to avoid, but instead to confront, to recall fully, and to reconstruct distressing current experiences and past memories. The true antithesis to intrusive reexperiencing is not freedom from trauma memories or trauma-related distress, but the capacity to choose whether, when, and how to recall and make sense of (i.e., emotionally and cognitively finding meaning in) those memories. This presupposes sophisticated emotion — and information — processing abilities that are precisely the mode of the "learning" brain that is overridden by post-traumatic stress-related survival reactions. Thus, authority over one's own memory (Harvey, 1996) may best be construed as the ability to choose whether, when, and how to recall memories (i.e., specific emotion and information processing skills) rather than purely reducing avoidance of traumatic memories (Ford, 2009).

- Body/Mind Work

  Developing a sense of bodily mastery and competence contradicts an identity of physical helplessness. . . Teaching terrified people to safely experience their sensations and emotions has not been given sufficient attention in mainstream trauma treatment . . . There is a long standing tradition of specific body-oriented treatment techniques, first articulated by Wilhelm Reich (1937), and in modern times expanded to trauma specific body-oriented work (e.g. Levine & Frederick, 1997, Gendlin, 1998), and psychodramatic techniques (e.g. Pesso & Crandell, 1991) focusing on experiencing, tolerating, and transforming trauma-related physical sensations (van der Kolk, 2001).

- Yoga, martial arts and self-defense courses like "model mugging" programs, Tai Chi, Qi Gong, drumming and chanting are brilliant options for creating body memories of competence and mastery. These experiences assist clients in "uncoupling" fear from excitement; uncoupling specific anxiety provoking physical sensations from their traumatic memories; and the development of feelings of mastery, competence and victory.

- EMDR and Somatic Experiencing for resolving traumatic material: Combining the procedures of Somatic Experiencing, i.e., focusing and tracking the client's "felt sense" with EMDR's alternating bilateral stimulation is an approach that (once adequately resourced) allows clients to safely "reprocess and/or renegotiate" traumatic material. This combination seems to facilitate rapid, adaptive, associative information processing regarding self and world, while simultaneously physically metabolizing and integrating bodily sensations and intense negative affects.

STAGE ONE:
STABILIZATION

STAGE ONE: STABILIZATION

CLINICAL ASSESSMENT AND DIAGNOSIS

Maladaptive Behaviors Three-Part Screening

The screening is meant for, well, screening. During the assessment phase, expecting full, accurate disclosure may be somewhat ambitious, but engaging a client in a conversation regarding the function that food, drugs, and alcohol play in coping with stress is a worthwhile endeavor. If the clinician genuinely understands (and can communicate to the client) that given the dearth of resources available, these coping strategies were far from "maladaptive"; they were the client's best efforts at managing what was — and likely still is — frequent, unmanageable emotional/affective states.

Illuminating the adaptive nature of each behavior — and the brilliance behind its utilization — is a not only a way to join with the client, but an opportunity for psychoeducation regarding the nature of trauma and its sequelae.

Beyond normalizing the behavior (with regards to symptom management), when the clinician explicates all of the benefits that each adaptation has provided the client, it is no longer necessary for the client to defend that behavior. Conversely, (s)he is now primed and free to identify and acknowledge the costs that each behavior has exacted.

CLIENT HANDOUT:
COPING BEHAVIORS SCREENING

DRUGS

Do you ever use drugs to calm down?	Yes	No
Do you ever use drugs to give you energy?	Yes	No
Do you use a combination of drugs at one time?	Yes	No
Is your drug use more than one day per week?	Yes	No
Do you have a history of using/abusing prescription drugs?	Yes	No
Have you attempted to quit your drug use, but been unsuccessful?	Yes	No
Do you feel guilty about your drug use?	Yes	No
Has your drug use ended relationships with friends?	Yes	No
Do you find yourself neglecting your family because of your drug use?	Yes	No
Has your drug use resulted in problems between you and your family members or friends?	Yes	No
Do your family members or friends ever complain about your drug use?	Yes	No
While under the influence of drugs, have you gotten into confrontations or fights with others?	Yes	No
Has your drug use ever contributed to you losing a job?	Yes	No
Has your drug use caused problems or gotten you into trouble at your workplace?	Yes	No
Have you ever gone to jail or been arrested for illegal drug possession?	Yes	No
Do you participate in illegal activities in order to get your drugs of choice?	Yes	No
When you stop taking your drug, do you experience any withdrawal symptoms or feel sick?	Yes	No
Has your drug use ever resulted in flashbacks or blackouts?	Yes	No
Have you ever had medical problems such as memory loss, hepatitis, convulsions, bleeding, etc., as a result of your drug use?	Yes	No
Have you sought help for your drug problem in the past?	Yes	No
Have you participated in any treatment programs related to your drug use?	Yes	No

COPING BEHAVIORS SCREENING, CONT.

ALCOHOL

Do you mostly drink in private or when you are alone?	**Yes**	**No**
Is there a particular time each day that you crave a drink?	**Yes**	**No**
Do you need "an eye opener" — a drink first thing in the morning in order to function?	**Yes**	**No**
Do you drink in order to forget about your difficulties and worries?	**Yes**	**No**
Do you have trouble sleeping because of your drinking?	**Yes**	**No**
Since you have begun drinking, are you less ambitious?	**Yes**	**No**
Does your drinking affect your home life for the worse?	**Yes**	**No**
Are you careless with your family's welfare when you are drinking?	**Yes**	**No**
Has your drinking caused financial problems for you and/or your family?	**Yes**	**No**
Do you feel regretful after you drink?	**Yes**	**No**
Have you ever "blacked out" or lost some memory — as a result of drinking?	**Yes**	**No**
Do you feel that drinking makes you feel more self-confidence?	**Yes**	**No**
When with others, do you tend to drink because you are anxious?	**Yes**	**No**
If you weren't drinking, would you be hanging out with the same crowd?	**Yes**	**No**
Do you have "a reputation" about your drinking?	**Yes**	**No**
Have you called in sick from work as a result of your drinking?	**Yes**	**No**
Has your job or participation in your workplace been negatively affected by your drinking?	**Yes**	**No**
Have you become less efficient since you started drinking?	**Yes**	**No**
Has your drinking ever resulted in the need for you to be hospitalized or institutionalized?	**Yes**	**No**
Have you sought treatment from a doctor or professional because of your drinking?	**Yes**	**No**

FOOD

I make excuses not to have to eat with my friends and/or family. (e.g. "I already ate," "I am not feeling well," etc.)	**Often**	**Sometimes**	**Rarely**	**Never**
My eating habits look different than those of my family and friends.	**Often**	**Sometimes**	**Rarely**	**Never**

I can't get through the day without worrying about what and how much I will eat?	**Often**	**Sometimes**	**Rarely**	**Never**
I prefer to eat alone or when I am sure that no one will see me.	**Often**	**Sometimes**	**Rarely**	**Never**
I binge eat, then throw up.	**Never**	**< 1/week**	**1–6/week**	**> 1/day**
I have rituals around eating, i.e., I cut my food into tiny pieces, hide it, spit it out, etc.	**Often**	**Sometimes**	**Rarely**	**Never**
I know what foods are "safe" for me to eat and what foods aren't.	**Often**	**Sometimes**	**Rarely**	**Never**
I hate when others show interest in what I eat and pressure me to eat more.	**Often**	**Sometimes**	**Rarely**	**Never**
I am afraid that no one would understand my fears about food and eating, so I keep these feelings to myself.	**Often**	**Sometimes**	**Rarely**	**Never**
I enjoy cooking meals and/or high calorie foods for others, but I can't or won't eat them.	**Often**	**Sometimes**	**Rarely**	**Never**
I have an overwhelming fear of gaining weight.			**True**	**False**
I can, and do, go through long periods of time without eating or eating very little.	**Often**	**Sometimes**	**Rarely**	**Never**
My friends tell me that I am thin, but I feel fat.	**Often**	**Sometimes**	**Rarely**	**Never**
I would panic if I found out that I gained weight.	**Almost Always**	**Sometimes**	**Rarely**	**Never**
I use laxatives, emetics, or diuretics to control my weight.	**Never**	**Rarely**	**Sometimes**	**Regularly**
(Females only) I don't get my period at all or I get it, but it's erratic			**True**	**False**
I exercise rigorously (at times excessively) to lose weight; I get anxious if I skip a workout.			**True**	**False**
It is important that I am thinner than my friends.	**Almost Always**	**Sometimes**	**Rarely**	**Never**
I can't maintain a "healthy weight" that's consistent with my build, age and height.			**True**	**False**
I spend a lot of time reading about dieting, exercising, fitness, or calorie counting.	**Often**	**Sometimes**	**Rarely**	**Never**

CLIENT HANDOUT:
TRAUMATIC STRESS INVENTORY

On a scale of 1–5, write the number that corresponds to how often you been "bothered by" the items below in the past month.

_____ Repeated, disturbing memories, thoughts, or images of a stressful experience from the past?

_____ Repeated, disturbing dreams of a stressful experience from the past?

_____ Suddenly acting or feeling as if a stressful experience were happening again (as if you were reliving it)?

_____ Feeling very upset when something reminded you of a stressful experience from the past?

_____ Having physical reactions (e.g., heart pounding, trouble breathing, or sweating) when something reminded you of a stressful experience from the past?

_____ Avoid thinking about or talking about a stressful experience from the past, or avoid having feelings related to it?

_____ Avoid activities or situations because they remind you of a stressful experience from the past?

_____ Trouble remembering important parts of a stressful experience from the past?

_____ Loss of interest in things that you used to enjoy?

_____ Feeling distant or cut off from other people?

_____ Feeling emotionally numb or being unable to have loving feelings for those close to you?

_____ Feeling as if your future will somehow be cut short?

_____ Trouble falling or staying asleep?

_____ Feeling irritable or having angry outbursts?

_____ Having difficulty concentrating?

_____ Being "super alert" or watchful on guard?

_____ Feeling jumpy or easily startled?

Score: _____

Traumatic Stress Inventory, Cont.

Description

The PCL is a 17-item self-report measure of the 17 DSM-IV symptoms of PTSD. Respondents rate how much they were "bothered by that problem in the past month." Items are rated on a 5-point scale ranging from 1 ("not at all") to 5 ("extremely"). There are several versions of the PCL. The original PCL is the PCL-M (military). The PCL-M asks about problems in response to "stressful military experiences." The PCL-S (specific) asks about problems in relation to an identified "stressful experience." The PCL-C (civilian) is for civilians and is not focused on any one traumatic event. Instead, it asks more generally about problems in relation to stressful experiences.

Scoring

The PCL can be scored in several different ways. A total score (range 17-85) can be obtained by summing the scores from each of the 17 items. Cutoff scores for a probable PTSD diagnosis have been validated for some populations, but may not generalize to other populations. A second way to score the PCL is to follow the DSM-IV criteria. It has been suggested that a combination of these two approaches (i.e., the requisite number of symptoms are endorsed within each cluster AND the total score is above the specified cut point for a specific population) may be best (for a detailed review, see Norris & Hamblen and Orsillo). Separate scores can also be obtained for Criteria B, C, and D. Behavioral Science Division, 1991. This is a Government document in the public domain.

Commercially Available Trauma Assessment Instruments

Traumatic Antecedents Questionnaire (TAQ)

This self-administered assessment tool gathers information about lifetime experiences in 10 domains: (1) competence, (2) safety, (3) neglect, (4) separations, (5) family secrets, (6) conflict resolution, (7) physical trauma, (8) sexual trauma, (9) witnessing trauma, and (10) exposure to drugs and alcohol. These domains are assessed at four different age periods: birth to 6 years, 7 to 12, 13 to 18, and adulthood. Thus, the TAQ provides invaluable information for guiding clinical inquiry and developmental formulations.

To Obtain Assessment Materials

Website: http://www.traumacenter.org/products/instruments.php
The Trauma Center at JRI
1269 Beacon Street, 1st Floor
Brookline, MA 02446
Phone: (617) 232-1303 x 204

Modified PTSD Symptom Scale

This scale is a 17-item questionnaire that asks patients to rate the frequency and intensity of symptoms in the past two weeks. Responses to the questions enable ratings of DSM-IV symptoms for PTSD, including (1) intrusions, (2) re-experiencing, (3) avoidance and numbing, and (4) increased arousal.

To Obtain Assessment Materials

Website: http://www.traumacenter.org/products/instruments.php
The Trauma Center at JRI
1269 Beacon Street, 1st Floor
Brookline, MA 02446
Phone: (617) 232-1303 x 204

STRUCTURED INTERVIEW FOR DISORDERS OF EXTREME STRESS (SIDES)
&
SELF-REPORT INSTRUMENT FOR DISORDERS OF EXTREME STRESS (SIDES-SR)

These 45-item scales assess presence and/or severity of the Disorders of Extreme Stress Not Otherwise Specified (DESNOS) diagnostic construct, which reflects the associated features of PTSD commonly seen in association with interpersonal stressors: impaired affect modulation; self-destructive and impulsive behavior; dissociative symptoms; somatic complaints; feelings of ineffectiveness, shame, despair, or hopelessness; feelings permanently damaged; a loss of previously sustained beliefs; hostility; social withdrawal; feeling constantly threatened; impaired relationships with others (DSM-IV, p. 425). The clinician-rater version was used for the DSM-IV Field Trials for PTSD, and has been validated as a measure of DESNOS diagnosis. The self-report version has good behavioral anchors and has demonstrated good internal reliability as a measure of current DESNOS severity. Both versions of the SIDES consist of six major scales with related subscales: (1) alteration in regulation of affect and impulses; (2) alterations in attention or consciousness; (3) alterations in self-perception; (4) alterations in relations with others; (5) somatization; (6) alterations in systems of meaning.

TO OBTAIN ASSESSMENT MATERIALS

Website: http://www.traumacenter.org/products/instruments.php
The Trauma Center at JRI
1269 Beacon Street, 1st Floor
Brookline, MA 02446
Phone: (617) 232-1303 x 204

TRAUMA FOCUSED INITIAL ADULT CLINICAL EVALUATION

This structured clinical interview was developed at the Trauma Center to facilitate a comprehensive intake for new patients. It focuses on trauma history and associated symptomatology with an emphasis on developmental, current internal resources, social supports, and substance abuse and treatment history. It is informed by empirical findings based on the TAQ, SIDES and PTSD instruments.

TO OBTAIN ASSESSMENT MATERIALS

Website: http://www.traumacenter.org/products/instruments.php
The Trauma Center at JRI
1269 Beacon Street, 1st Floor
Brookline, MA 02446
Phone: (617) 232-1303 x 204

Trauma Symptom Inventory (TSI)

The TSI is used in the evaluation of acute and chronic post-traumatic symptomatology, including the effects of rape, spouse abuse, physical assault, combat experiences, major accidents, and natural disasters, as well as the lasting sequelae of childhood abuse and other early traumatic events. The various scales of the TSI assess a wide range of psychological impacts. These include not only symptoms typically associated with post-traumatic stress disorder (PTSD) or acute stress disorder (ASD), but also those intra — and interpersonal difficulties often associated with more chronic psychological trauma.

MEASURE CONTENT: The 100 items of the TSI are contained in a reusable test booklet. Respondents complete a separate answer sheet that facilitates rapid scoring. Each symptom item is rated according to its frequency of occurrence over the prior six months, using a four-point scale ranging from 0 ("never") to 3 ("often"). The TSI does not generate DSM-IV diagnoses; instead, it is intended to evaluate the relative level of various forms of post-traumatic distress. The clinical scales are:

- **Anxious Arousal** (AA) (symptoms of anxiety, including those associated with post-traumatic hyperarousal);

- **Depression** (D) (depressive symptomatology, both in terms of mood state and depressive cognitive distortions);

- **Anger/Irritability** (AI) (angry or irritable affect, as well as associated angry cognitions and behavior);

- **Intrusive Experiences** (IE) (intrusive symptoms associated with post-traumatic stress, such as flashbacks, nightmares, and intrusive thoughts);

- **Defensive Avoidance** (DA) (post-traumatic avoidance, both cognitive and behavioral);

- **Dissociation** (DIS) (dissociative symptomatology, such as depersonalization, out-of-body experiences, and psychic numbing);

- **Sexual Concerns** (SC) (sexual distress, such as sexual dissatisfaction, sexual dysfunction, and unwanted sexual thoughts or feelings);

- **Dysfunctional Sexual Behavior** (DSB) (sexual behavior that is in some way dysfunctional, either because of its indiscriminate quality, its potential for self-harm, or its inappropriate use to accomplish non-sexual goals);

- **Impaired Self-reference** (ISR) (problems in the "self" domain, such as identity confusion, self-other disturbance, and a relative lack of self-support);

- **Tension Reduction Behavior** (TRB) (the respondent's tendency to turn to external methods of reducing internal tension or distress, such as self-mutilation, angry outbursts, and suicide threats).

To Obtain Assessment Materials

Website: http://www.johnbriere.com/tsi.htm
Psychological Assessment Resources, Inc.
P.O. Box 998, Odessa, FL, 33556
Phone: 1-800-331-TEST

PERSONALITY ASSESSMENT INVENTORY™ (PAI®)

This objective inventory of adult personality assesses psychopathological syndromes and provides information relevant for clinical diagnosis, treatment planning, and screening for psychopathology. Since its introduction, the PAI has been heralded as one of the most important innovations in the field of clinical assessment.

PAI® SCALES AND SUBSCALES

The 344 PAI items constitute 22 nonoverlapping scales covering the constructs most relevant to a broad-based assessment of mental disorders: 4 validity scales, 11 clinical scales, 5 treatment scales, and 2 interpersonal scales. To facilitate interpretation and to cover the full range of complex clinical constructs, 10 scales contain conceptually derived subscales.

The Treatment scales: two indicators of potential for harm to self or others; two measures of the respondent's environmental circumstances and one indicator of the respondent's motivation for treatment.

The Interpersonal scales were developed to provide an assessment of the respondent's interpersonal style along two dimensions: a warm affiliative versus a cold rejecting style and a dominating/controlling versus a meek, submissive style. The PAI includes a Borderline Features scale and an Antisocial Features scale. Both of these scales specifically assess character pathology. The Borderline Features scale is the only PAI scale that has four subscales, reflecting the factorial complexity of the construct. The Antisocial Features scale includes a total of three facets: one assessing antisocial behaviors, and the other two assessing antisocial traits.

TO OBTAIN ASSESSMENT MATERIALS

Website: http://www3.parinc.com/products/product.aspx?Productid=PAI
Psychological Assessment Resources (PAR)
P.O. Box 998, Odessa, FL, 33556

THE DISSOCIATIVE EXPERIENCES SCALE, II (DES,II)

The DES is a brief, self-report measure of the frequency of dissociative experiences. The scale was developed to provide a reliable, valid, and convenient way to quantify dissociative experiences. The Dissociative Experiences Scale (DES) was developed by Eve Bernstein Carlson, Ph.D. and Frank W. Putnam, M.D. The overall DES score is obtained by adding up the 28 item scores and dividing by 28: this yields an overall score ranging from 0 to 100 DES is not a diagnostic instrument; it is a screening instrument. Copies of the DES and the A-DES are copyright-free. You are welcome to photocopy any of the materials for use in research or clinical work. You do not need special permission to use the DES in your research or clinical work. Copies of the DES are packaged with reprints of the article, an update on the Dissociative Experiences Scale (Dissociation 6 (1):16-27), which is a manual for the DES, and a list of 333 references for studies that have used or discussed the use of the DES as a measure of dissociation.

TO OBTAIN ASSESSMENT MATERIALS

Website: http://www.sidran.org/store/
Email: orders@sidran.org

CLINICIAN'S CORNER:
SUICIDE: NATIONAL STATISTICS

First things first. The common adage, "Where there is life, there is hope" should, and does, provide comfort and encouragement to many people. However, since its opposite is also true, our first priority should address keeping our clients alive. Here are the national statistics:

GENERAL

- Over 32,000 people in the United States die by suicide every year.
- In 2005 (latest available data), there were > 32,000 reported suicide deaths.
- Suicide is the fourth leading cause of death for adults between the ages of 18 and 65 years in the U.S., with approximately 26,500 suicides.
- Currently, suicide is the 11th leading cause of death in the United States.
- A person dies by suicide about every 16 minutes in the United States.
- An attempt is estimated to be made once every minute.
- Ninety percent of all people who die by suicide have a diagnosable psychiatric disorder at the time of their death.
- There are four male suicides for every female suicide, but twice as many females as males attempt suicide.

YOUTH

- Suicide is the fifth leading cause of death among those 5-14 years old
- Suicide is the third leading cause of death among those 15-24 years old
- Risk factors for suicide among the young include:
  a. suicidal thoughts
  b. psychiatric disorders (such as depression, impulsive aggressive behavior, bipolar disorder, certain anxiety disorders)
  c. drug and/or alcohol abuse

    d. previous suicide attempts

    e. increased risk with situational stress

    f. increased risk with access to firearms

OLDER PEOPLE

- The suicide rates for men rise with age, most significantly after age 65

- The rate of suicide in men 65+ is seven times that of females who are 65+

- The suicide rates for women peak between the ages of 45–54 years old, and again after age 75

- > 30 percent of patients suffering from major depression report suicidal ideation

- Risk factors for suicide among the elderly include: a previous attempt, the presence of a mental illness, the presence of a physical illness, social isolation (some studies have shown this is especially so in older males who are recently widowed) and access to means, such as the availability of firearms in the home

DEPRESSION AND ALCOHOL

- Over 60 percent of all people who die by suicide suffer from major depression. If one includes alcoholics who are depressed, this figure rises to over 75 percent

- Depression affects nearly 10 percent of Americans ages 18 and over in a given year

- Thirty percent of all clinically depressed patients attempt suicide; half of them ultimately die by suicide

- Depression is among the most treatable of psychiatric illnesses

- Alcoholism is a factor in about 30 percent of all completed suicides

- Ninety-six percent of alcoholics who die by suicide continued their substance abuse up to the end of their lives

Figures from the National Center for Health Statistics for the year 2005

CLINICIAN'S CORNER:
SUICIDE: DISCUSSION

"To be, or not to be: that is the question:
Whether 'tis nobler in the mind to suffer
The slings and arrows of outrageous fortune,
Or to take arms against a sea of troubles,
And by opposing end them? To die: to sleep;
No more; and by a sleep to say we end
The heart-ache and the thousand natural shocks
That flesh is heir to, 'tis a consummation
Devoutly to be wish'd. To die, to sleep;
To sleep: perchance to dream: ay, there's the rub;
For in that sleep of death what dreams may come
When we have shuffled off this mortal coil."

—William Shakespeare, *Hamlet*

To state the obvious, suicidal clients are in crisis. Crisis is a time for clinicians to rally — to use any and all means at his/her disposal to keep the client alive. In an interview with David Van Nuy, Marsha Linehan said, "When it comes to suicide, you really can not put that off and say, 'well, we'll just accept that you're killing yourself' because the person will be dead and the treatment won't work if they're dead. No treatment works with dead people. So, we focus first on life interfering behavior and that's the main target of the treatment. Only if we think the person is going to be alive, by the next week do we target anything else."

Most clinicians may be a bit less irreverent than Dr. Linehan with regards to discussing suicide with clients; however, avoidance of the subject is much more costly — for clients and clinicians. Some clinicians choose not to broach the subject at all; they avoid administering screening questionnaires or directly inquiring about suicide — fearing that their clients might find such questions distasteful, embarrassing, or worse, that such questions may lead a client to suicidal thoughts (Hirschfeld and Russell, 1997). Avoiding questions regarding suicidal thoughts or behaviors because of perceived liability risks is a bad clinical decision based on an erroneous premise. Clinicians should be aware that not only is it an erroneous premise, but its converse is factual; clinicians may be held liable if suicidal intentions were suspected and the clinician neglected to ask about suicidal thoughts or behavior and/or failed to document patient's response to such questions (*see* Bongar, 1991 for review).

To allay some of the warranted and unwarranted fear, the research suggests that although most clients may be reluctant to raise the issue of suicide on their own (Kaplan, Anix, Sanderson, Keswani, deLecuona, and Joseph, 1994), they are, in fact, willing to discuss their suicidal thinking if given the opportunity. The bad news is that even when clinicians are willing and able to engage clients in the discussion of suicide, accurately predicting if and when a client is at risk is still very challenging. The good news is that we know the risk factors, and when considered in context they offer clinicians some guidance in more accurately assessing risk.

The following is a series of interview questions regarding suicide: ideation, intent, lethality, motivation and the presence of a viable plan, followed by two empirically validated screening instruments. The first instrument — produced by a task force for the American Association of Suicidology (*cf.* Rudd, *et al,* 2006) — is a list of warning signs for suicide summarized by the acronym, IS PATH WARM. The second instrument — originally described by Patterson, et al-is is checklist of risk factors with a simple scoring system based on the total number of items endorsed by the client. It is summarized by the acronym, SAD PERSONS.

SUICIDE ASSESSMENT QUESTIONS

When your principles seem to be demanding suicide, clearly it's time to check your premises.

— Nathaniel Branden, The Free Radical, Oct. 2004

IDEATION

1. Are you having suicidal thoughts/feelings now?
2. Are they active/volitional or passive/non-volitional?
   a. When did they begin?
   b. How frequent are they?
   c. How persistent are they?
   d. How obsessive are they?
3. Have you had them today?
4. During the past week?
5. What are the thoughts?
6. What do you do when the thoughts/feelings come?
7. Can you control them? When have you in the past? How?

MOTIVATION

1. What motivates your wish to die?
2. Is the motivation to hurt someone else as well?
3. Is the motivation to escape?
4. Is the motivation to punish yourself?
5. What would motivate you to continue living?
6. What/who is your main reason for living?
7. What is your view of death?
8. Positive/Negative?
9. What does the possibility of death hold for you?
10. What do you think happens after you die?

SUPPORT SYSTEM

1. Do you have significant people in your life?
2. Has a significant person ever left you?
3. Has a significant person ever threatened to leave you?
4. Has there been an interruption in your treatment/therapy?
5. Has there been a disruption in your support system?

SUICIDE PLAN

1. How far has your suicide planning process proceeded?
2. Have you chosen a specific method?
3. Where will you carry out the planned suicide?
4. When will you carry out the suicide?
5. Do you have the available means to carry it out?
6. Have you planned the sequence of events?
7. What is the intended goal? (e.g. death, self-injury, or another outcome)
8. Is it likely that someone will find you before it is accomplished?
9. What preparations have you made?
10. Have you rehearsed for suicide?
11. Have you attempted suicide previously?
12. What happened?
13. Was that what you wanted to happen?
14. Did anything unforeseen happen?

SELF–INFLICTED VIOLENCE

1. Have you engaged in self-inflicted violence?
2. How do you calm yourself down?
3. Do you have a history of impulsive behavior?

DEPRESSION/HOPELESSNESS

1. On a scale of 1–10, where 0 is not at all depressed and 10 is the most depressed that you've ever felt, how do you feel now?
2. On a scale of 1–10, where 0 is not at all hopeless and 10 is the most hopeless that you've ever felt, how do you feel now?

RECENT STRESSORS

1. Have there been recent stressors in your life?
2. Are you facing a loss, disappointment, humiliation or failure?
3. Are you willing to engage in treatment?

"IS PATH WARM"
AND "SAD PERSONS"

- Ideation (expressing the idea of suicide; threatening or talking about it; etc.)
- Substance Abuse
- Several emotions: purposelessness, anxiety, trapped, hopelessness, withdrawal, anger, recklessness and mood change

IS PATH WARM
I = Ideation
S = Substance Abuse
P = Purposelessness
A = Anxiety
T = Trapped
H = Hopelessness
W = Withdrawal
A = Anger
R = Recklessness
M = Mood Changes

WARNING SIGNS OF ACUTE RISK

1. Threatening to hurt or kill him/herself
2. Talking about wanting to hurt or kill him/herself
3. Looking for means to kill him/herself, e.g., seeking access to firearms, available pills, or other means
4. Talking or writing about death, dying, or suicide (out of the ordinary).
5. Increased substance (alcohol or drug) use
6. No reason for living; no sense of purpose in life
7. Anxiety, agitation, insomnia, or hypersomnia
8. Feeling trapped — like there's no way out
9. Hopelessness
10. Withdrawal from friends, family, and society
11. Rage, uncontrolled anger, seeking revenge
12. Acting reckless or engaging in risky activities, seemingly without thinking
13. Dramatic mood changes

SAD PERSONS

Give one point for each positive answer:

S	1	Sex — Although women make twice as many attempts, men complete suicide about four times more often. (Give one point if male.)
A	1	Age (see table below*)
D	1	Depression — The suicide rate for those who are clinically depressed is about 20 times greater than for the general population. Hopelessness is one aspect of depression that has a close tie to suicide. These two issues, depression and hopelessness, are the strongest predictors of desire to die.
P	1	Prior History — Roughly 80% of completed suicides were preceded by a prior attempt.
E	1	Ethanol Abuse: Alcohol and/or drug abuse increase risk
R	1	Rational thinking loss
S	1	Support system loss
O	1	Organized plan
N	1	No significant other
S	1	Sickness

Score _____

Score	Risk for Suicide
0-2	Low threat presently, continue present treatment
3-4	Send home, arrange for client to be monitored frequently
5-6	Consider hospitalization involuntary or voluntary, depending on your level of comfort and certainty that your client will return for another session
7-10	Without a doubt hospitalize voluntarily or involuntarily

Age	# of Suicides	Rate
5–14	272	0.7
15-24	4,212	10.0
25-34	4,990	12.4
35-44	6,550	14.9
45-54	6,991	16.5
55-64	4,210	13.9
65-74	2,344	12.6
75-84	2,200	16.9
85+	860	16.9
Total	32,637	11.0

Clients with a suicide plan, access to lethal means, recent social stressors and symptoms indicative of a psychiatric diagnosis should be hospitalized immediately!

If the client is cooperative and willing to be hospitalized,

1. His/her family should be informed of the decision to hospitalize.

2. (S)he should not be left unaccompanied at any time during transfer to a higher level of care.

> GROUNDS FOR INVOLUNTARY COMMITMENT
>
> - Imminent danger to self or others
> - An inability to care for oneself

3. If suicidal client is intoxicated, psychotic, or unknown to the clinician, (s)he should be promptly and securely transported to the nearest crisis center.

If the client is uncooperative and/or unwilling to be hospitalized,

1. Involuntary commitment should be sought.

2. When unsure of the steps to take, a crisis center or emergency-department psychiatrist should be enlisted.

3. In most states, procedures are in place to allow for an involuntary hospitalization of 24 to 120 hours before a hearing is held with a judge to extend the hospitalization.

In addition to the crisis plans and safety contracts found in the next section of the workbook, an additional tactic available to the clinician in an emergency is to ask the client to sign or verbally agree to a "time-limited 'no harm' contract." In the contract, the client agrees to refrain from harming him/herself for a specific, brief time period (e.g., 24 to 48 hours). If the situation changes, then the client also agrees to contact the clinician. In essence, clients aren't coerced into not harming themselves; they are coerced into negotiating an agreement to refrain from harming themselves until they have spoken to the clinician. In the contract, it is explicated that the clinician and/or family member(s)/friend(s) will follow-up by telephone and/or in-person. When the contract expires, the situation should be reevaluated and renewed for another agreed upon time period.

The ongoing assessment of suicidal ideation and behavior provides important safeguards for managing high-risk patients. Several measures have been designed for repeated use during an intervention trial, such as the Self-Monitoring Suicide Ideation Scale (Clum and Curtin, 1993) or Linehan's diary card of monitoring suicide ideation and self-harm behaviors (Linehan, 1993). In addition, the suicide item and hopelessness item from the Beck Depression Inventory-II (BDI-II; Beck, Steer, and Brown, 1996) may also be used to monitor changes in suicidality on a regular basis during the course of treatment. Patients attending outpatient CBT, for example, typically complete the BDI-II prior to each visit. If either the suicide or hopelessness items are endorsed, then the clinician may conduct a detailed assessment of suicide risk and provide appropriate therapeutic interventions to reduce a patient's suicidality (see Ellis and Newman, 1998).

Additional measurement instruments may be obtained by contacting the authors below:

SELF-MONITORING SUICIDE IDEATION SCALE

TO OBTAIN ASSESSMENT MATERIALS

George A. Clum
Psychology
5093G Derring Hall
Blacksburg, VA 24061
E-Mail: gclum@vt.edu

BECK DEPRESSION INVENTORY – II

TO OBTAIN ASSESSMENT MATERIALS

Aaron T. Beck
University of Pennsylvania
The Science Center, Room 754
3600 Market Street
Philadelphia, PA 19104-2648
E-Mail: becka@landru.pcr.upenn.edu

SAD PERSONS SCALE

TO OBTAIN ASSESSMENT MATERIALS

W.M. Patterson
Smolian Clinic
Room 210
Department of Psychiatry
University Station
Birmingham, AL 15294

LIFETIME PARASUICIDE COUNT, LINEHAN REASONS FOR LIVING INVENTORY, AND SUICIDE BEHAVIORS QUESTIONNAIRE REVISED

TO OBTAIN ASSESSMENT MATERIALS

Marsha M. Linehan
Behavioral Research & Therapy Clinics
Department of Psychology Box 351525
University of Washington
Seattle, Washington 98195
E-Mail: linehan@u.washington.edu

HOTLINE: NATIONAL SUICIDE PREVENTION LIFELINE AT (800) 273-TALK (8255)

- **Suicide Prevention Resource Center** (http://www.sprc.org). The Suicide Prevention Resource Center (SPRC) provides prevention support, training, and materials to strengthen suicide prevention efforts. Among the resources found on its website is the SPRC Library Catalog (http://library.sprc.org), a searchable database containing a wealth of information on suicide and suicide prevention, including publications, peer-reviewed research studies, curricula, and web-based resources.

- **American Association of Suicidology** (http://www.suicidology.org). The American Association of Suicidology is a nonprofit organization dedicated to the understanding and prevention of suicide. It promotes research, public awareness programs, public education, and training for professionals and volunteers and serves as a national clearinghouse for information on suicide.

- **American Foundation for Suicide Prevention** (http://www.afsp.org). The American Foundation for Suicide Prevention (AFSP) is dedicated to advancing our knowledge of suicide and our ability to prevent it. AFSP's activities include supporting research projects; providing information and education about depression and suicide; promoting professional education for the recognition and treatment of depressed and suicidal individuals.

- **National Center for Injury Prevention and Control** (http://www.cdc.gov/ncipc). The National Center for Injury Prevention and Control (NCIPC), located at the Centers for Disease Control and Prevention, is a valuable source of information and statistics about suicide, suicide risk, and suicide prevention. To locate information on suicide and suicide prevention, scroll down the left-hand navigation bar on the NCIPC website and click on "Suicide" under the "Violence" heading.

- **National Suicide Prevention Lifeline** (http://www.suicidepreventionlifeline.org). The National Suicide Prevention Lifeline provides immediate assistance to individuals in suicidal crisis by connecting them to the nearest available suicide prevention and mental health service provider through a toll-free telephone number: (800) 273-TALK (8255). Technical assistance, training, and other resources are available to the crisis centers and mental health service providers that participate in the network of services linked to the National Suicide Prevention Lifeline.

- **Suicide Prevention Action Network USA** (http://www.spanusa.org). Suicide Prevention Action Network USA (SPAN USA) is the nation's only suicide prevention organization dedicated to leveraging grassroots support among suicide survivors (those who have lost a loved one to suicide) and others to advance public policies that help prevent suicide.

- **Go Ask Alice!** (http://www.goaskalice.columbia.edu) is a web-based health question-and-answer service produced by Alice!, Columbia University's Health Education Program. Go Ask Alice! provides information to help young people make better decisions concerning their health and well-being. Go Ask Alice! answers questions about relationships, sexuality, emotional health, alcohol and other drugs, and other topics. The addresses of e-mails sent to Go Ask Alice! are electronically scrambled to preserve the senders' confidentiality. Questions are answered by a team of Columbia University health educators and information and research specialists from other health-related organizations.

- **Samaritans** (http://www.samaritans.org) is an organization based in the United Kingdom that offers 24-hour, confidential emotional support to people who are experiencing feelings of distress or despair, including those feelings that may lead to suicide. The Samaritans operate a free and confidential e-mail service, which generally responds to your e-mail within 24 hours. You can send an e-mail to jo@samaritans.org or use the Samaritans website to send a confidential e-mail that cannot be traced back to your address.

- **Ulifeline.org** (http://www.ulifeline.org) is a web-based resource created by the Jed Foundation to provide students with a non-threatening and supportive link to their college's mental health center as well as important mental health information. Students are able to download information about various mental illnesses, ask questions, make appointments, and seek help anonymously via the Internet.

CLINICIAN'S CORNER: Crisis

These then are my last words to you. Be not afraid of life. Believe that life is worth living and your belief will help create the fact.

— William James

Introduction

This is your plan. Develop it when you are feeling well. Take time to make good decisions for your plan; work at it for a while, then leave it for several days and keep coming back to it until you have developed a plan you feel has the best chance of working for you. Collaborate with psychiatrist, therapist, family members and other folks on your support team. Once you have completed your crisis plan, give a copy to the people you name in this plan as your supporters.

Symptoms: Describe symptoms that indicate to your support team that they need to step in and help. Although this may be difficult to do, a careful, well-developed description of symptoms that you know would indicate to you that you can't make good decisions anymore, you can stay in control even when things seem to be out of control. Allow yourself plenty of time to complete this section. Ask your friends, family members, and other supporters for input, but always remember that the final determination is up to you.

> ### Things to Remember
>
> Crises are temporary!
>
> This is your plan
>
> Develop it when you are feeling well
>
> Don't rush it
>
> Be clear and Specific
>
> Collaborate
>
> Share it with your support team

Remember, crises are temporary!

Be very clear and specific in describing each symptom. Don't just summarize; spell it out. Your list of symptoms might include:

- Neglecting personal hygiene (for how many days?)
- Not understanding what people are saying
- Not knowing who I am

- Not knowing/ recognizing family members and friends
- Uncontrollable pacing; inability to stay still
- Self-inflicted violence (degree)
- Being abusive, destructive, or violent toward others or property
- Abusing alcohol and/or drugs
- Not getting out of bed (for how long?)
- Refusing to eat or drink

This is a sample crisis plan worksheet. There is a blank one immediately following it.

Symptoms that indicate that I need help:

1. *Cutting myself on arms and face.*
2. *Staying in bed more than 24 hours.*
3. *Eating only once a day.*
4.
5.
6.

List any prescription medications, vitamins, herbs, alternative medications (such as homeopathic remedies), and supplements you are currently taking:

Current Medication	Current Dosage
Effexor	*150mg/QAM*
Propranalol	*10mg, 2*day*
Restoril	*.5mg at night*

List medications that should be avoided—like those you are allergic to, that conflict with another medication, or cause undesirable side effects. Note which should be increased or decreased if you are in crisis, and which you have discovered are not good for you:

Medications that have helped in a crisis	Medications that made me worse
Seroquel 25mg at night	
Ativan .5mg for panic	

SUPPORT TEAM

1. List the people who you want to take over for you when the symptoms you listed in the previous section arise. Before listing people in this part of your plan though, talk with them about what you'd like from them and make sure they understand and agree to be in the plan. They can be family members, friends, or health care providers. They should be committed to following the plans you have written. When you first develop this plan, your list may be mostly health care providers. But as you work on developing your support system, try to add more family members and friends because they will be more available.

2. It's best to have at least five people on your list of supporters. If you don't have that many supporters now, you may need to work on developing new and/or closer relationships with people.

3. Who do you want involved? Who do you not want involved?

4. List physician, psychiatrist, pharmacist, family members, friends, therapist, case manager and other health care providers, along with their phone numbers:

	Name	Relationship	Phone #
1.	Dr. Kellogg	Psychiatrist	610-557-9870
2.	Mary	Therapist	487-449-2677
3.	Gerry Stipe	Friend	215-786-8027
4.	Jimmy Simms	Brother	215-918-9836
5.	John Carroll	Case Manager	215-633-8936
6.			

SUPPORT

What do you need from others? What does support look like? Describe what your supporters can do for you that will be helpful and you feel better. This part of the plan is very important and deserves careful attention. Describe everything you can think of that you want your supporters to do for you. Include the things that you do not want others to do for you—things they might otherwise do because they think it would be helpful, but that might even be harmful or worsen the situation.

Helpful (Things Others Can Do)	Not Helpful (Things Others Should Avoid Doing)
Listen to me without giving me advice, judging me, or criticizing me.	*Taking away my cigarettes and/or coffee.*
Give me stuff to draw or paint.	*Telling me . . . it's all in my head or it's all good.*
Play video games with me.	*Talking too much or too loud.*
Make sure I take my vitamins and other medications.	*Forcing me to do anything*
Hold me fairly tightly and tell me I'm OK and you're not leaving.	*Telling me to snap out of it; get over it, etc.*
Remind me to play the guided imagery. Make sure I have my iPod.	

If I require hospitalization, these are the acceptable and unacceptable facilities:

Preferred Treatment Facilities	Treatment Facilities to be Avoided
Bryn Mawr Psychiatric Unit	*Hell Hole State Hospital*
Sheppard-Pratt	

RECOMMENDATIONS:

Copy following pages and co-create a Crisis/Safety Plan with client in session. Request that client sign and date Crisis/Safety Plan, knowing that this Plan/Contract is indicative of a relational agreement — not just a piece of paper.

CLIENT HANDOUT:
CRISIS PLAN (LONG FORM)

1. **Introduction:** This is your plan. Develop it when you are feeling well. Take time to make good decisions for your plan; work at it for a while, then leave it for several days and keep coming back to it until you have developed a plan you feel has the best chance of working for you. Collaborate with psychiatrist, therapist, family members and other folks on your support team. Once you have completed your crisis plan, give a copy to the people you name in this plan as your supporters.

2. **Symptoms:** Describe symptoms that indicate to your support team that they need to step in and help. Remember, crises are temporary! Be very clear and specific in describing each symptom. Don't just summarize; spell it out.

SYMPTOMS THAT INDICATE THAT I NEED HELP:

1. _____

2. _____

3. _____

4. _____

5. _____

6. _____

7. _____

CRISIS PLAN (LONG FORM), CONT.

List any prescription medications, vitamins, herbs, alternative medications (such as homeopathic remedies), and supplements you are currently taking:

Current Medication	Current Dosage
_____	_____
_____	_____
_____	_____
_____	_____
_____	_____
_____	_____

List medications that should be avoided—like those you are allergic to, that conflict with another medication, or cause undesirable side effects. Note which should be increased or decreased if you are in crisis, and which you have discovered are not good for you:

Medications that have helped in a crisis	Medications that made me worse
_____	_____
_____	_____
_____	_____
_____	_____

Crisis Plan (Long Form), Cont.

List the people who you want to take over for you when the symptoms you listed in the previous section arise. Before listing people in this part of your plan though, talk with them about what you'd like from them and make sure they understand and agree to be in the plan. Who do you want involved? Who do you not want involved?

List physician, psychiatrist, pharmacist, family members, friends, therapist, case manager and other health care providers, along with their phone numbers:

	Name	**Relationship**	**Phone #**
1.	_____	_____	_____
2.	_____	_____	_____
3.	_____	_____	_____
4.	_____	_____	_____
5.	_____	_____	_____
6.	_____	_____	_____

What do you need from others? What does support look like? Describe what your supporters can do for you that will be helpful and make you feel better. This part of the plan is very important and deserves careful attention. Describe everything you can think of that you want your supporters to do for you. Include the things that you do not want others to do for you—things they might otherwise do because they think it would be helpful, but that might even be harmful or worsen the situation.

Helpful **(Things Others Can Do)**	**Not Helpful** **(Things Others Should Avoid Doing)**

CRISIS PLAN (LONG FORM), CONT.

If I require hospitalization, these are the acceptable and unacceptable facilities:

Preferred Treatment Facilities	Treatment Facilities to be Avoided

Update the plan when you learn new information or change your mind about things. Date your crisis plan each time you change it and give revised copies to your supporters.

CLIENT HANDOUT:
CRISIS PLAN (SHORT FORM)

THINGS TO DO WHEN I FEEL UNSAFE (IN ORDER):

1. _____

2. _____

3. _____

4. _____

5. _____

6. _____

7. _____

8. _____

9. _____

10. _____

11. _____

12. _____

13. _____

14. _____

15. _____

CLINICIAN'S CORNER:
SELF-INFLICTED VIOLENCE: IT'S ALL ABOUT COPING

You may be unfamiliar with this type of coping, or you may understand it completely. When faced with it, you may feel terrified, mortified, sad, and/or angry. Below is a basic primer regarding SIV, its function, clinician attitudes, and best practice for dealing with clients who self-injure. Immediately following this section is a client packet including client worksheets and safety contract.

Here are the basics:

It's called lots of thing: self-inflicted violence, self-injury, self-harm, parasuicide, self-abuse and self-mutilation (this last one seems to particularly annoy people who use this style of coping). The forms and severity of self-injury vary, but the most commonly seen acts are:

Cutting	Scratching	Abrasions/Bruising
Burning	Branding	Hitting
Head-Banging	Marking	Picking Skin
Carving	Biting	Pulling Hair

It's not self-injury if the primary purpose is:

- Sexual gratification, body decoration (e.g., body piercing, tattooing)
- Spiritual enlightenment via ritual, fitting in, or being cool

How many?

It is estimated that self-injurers represent nearly one percent of the population, with a higher proportion of females than males. The typical onset of self-harming acts is at puberty. The behaviors often last for five to ten years, but can persist much longer without appropriate treatment.

What feelings about — and reactions to — arise when you encounter a person who is or has been hurting him/herself?

_____

_____

_____

Write down your own reactions and reactions that you may have heard from your colleagues regarding clients who self injure:

_____

_____

_____

But Why?!

Some explanations from some real people:

I do it because I can't talk to anyone about how I'm feeling. The night is really bad for me and that is when I have the most problems with hurting myself. I have nightmares about my past when I was in an abusive relationship. I have tried lots of self-help stuff, but some nights I just can't help it. I wish I could tell someone, but I don't think I can.

> Female, age 21, 5 years SIB, college sophomore

I do it for different reasons, depending on what state of mind I am in. I will do it sometimes as a way to get relief from the pain I am feeling inside. Other times I do because at the time I feel I deserve to be punished. And other times I do it to "shout out" to the world that I need help and it is this bad.

> Female, age 38, 27 years SIB, some college

I do not know why I cut, but it scares the hell out of me. Most of the time I am feeling very rejected or angry or I am seething with self-hatred. I do not cut for attention or to create dramatics. When I engage in this behavior, it is always alone and I have never told anyone about it.

> Female, age 33, SIB since teens, Ph.D.

I feel like "Now they'll know by God! Surely they can see how much pain I'm in now." I also feel anger and hatred while I'm doing it. Usually just at the whole world. Afterwards I tend to think "Well, I hope this works." Of course it never does because no one ever finds out how the cut really got there."

"I feel like I'm in control of my life, not everyone else. I have the ULTIMATE control. I don't deserve death, but I don't deserve to be healthy, as I am. I need to feel the pain."

> Female, SIB since age 26, AA in nursing

To punish myself for being a bad person. To feel the pain that is inside physically. To see my pain and show to myself it is real. To injure myself and cause myself harm. To show to myself that no one else can hurt me more than I can hurt myself. I never had anything that terrible happen to me and my childhood problems are minor so I don't understand why I feel I have to self-harm. Never been explained by a psychiatrist. Never had a diagnosis. Told I'm not mentally ill and that is all.

Female, age 28, 3 years SIB

BUT ISN'T THAT JUST CRAZY?

Let's be candid, is it any more crazy than drowning sorrows in a bottle of Absolut?

It's a coping mechanism; it is just not one that is as understandable or acceptable to society as alcoholism, drug abuse, overeating, anorexia and bulimia, workaholism, smoking cigarettes, and/or other forms of problem avoidance.

IT'S ALL ABOUT COPING

People generally do things for reasons that make sense to them. These reasons may not make sense to you, but they exist, and recognizing them is crucial to understanding why clients inflict violence upon themselves. Once you understand the reasons behind a particular act of self-harm then you know which coping skills your client is lacking. Once you know what skills your client is lacking, then you can collaborate with the client in order to develop those skills.

The erroneous assumption that the alternative to self-injury is "acting normally," is, in fact, wrong . . . the alternative to self-injury is total loss of control and possibly suicide. It becomes a forced choice from among limited options. (Solomon and Farrand, 1996)

PSYCHOLOGICAL MOTIVATIONS FOR SIV FALL IN THREE MAIN CATEGORIES:

1. Affect regulation
2. Communication
3. Control/punishment

Affect Regulation: Bringing the body back to equilibrium in the face of turbulent or unsettling feelings, including:

- Calming of the body in times of high emotional and physiological arousal
- Reconnecting with the body after a dissociative episode
- Validating the inner pain with an outer expression
- Avoiding suicide because of unbearable feelings

Communication: If/when the communication is directed at others, the injury is often seen as manipulative, however, it's more of a way to express things that cannot be spoken.

Control/Punishment includes:

- Bargaining and magical thinking (if I hurt myself, then the bad thing I am fearing will be prevented)

- Self-control (overlaps somewhat with affect regulation; in fact, most of the reasons for self-harm listed above have an element of affect modulation in them).

- Protecting other people

- Trauma Reenactment: Miller (1995) suggests that many self-harmers suffer from what she calls Trauma Reenactment Syndrome, positing that women who've been traumatized suffer a sort of internal split of consciousness; when they go into a self-harming episode, their conscious and subconscious minds take on three roles: the abuser (the one who harms), the victim, and the non-protecting bystander.

Four common characteristics:

1. A sense of being at war with their bodies ("my body, my enemy")

2. Excessive secrecy as a guiding principle of life

3. Inability to self-protect (often seen in a specific kind of fragmentation of self)

4. Relationships dominated by a struggle for control. (Miller, D. 1995 *Women Who Hurt Themselves: A Book Of Hope And Understanding,* Basic Books, NY, NY)

RECOMMENDATION

If your client is willing to address self-inflicted violence, copy the following pages and give him/her the "SIV packet." Like all assessment instruments, it is also an intervention. Have client read and decide if this something that (s)he is ready to begin. Co-create a plan by developing strategies, identifying and introducing alternative coping methods, and developing increased support.

The following is an excerpt from the upcoming book, *A Rough Couple of Days: the Narcissistic Therapist and the Borderline Client.* It is a client and clinician's account of self-disclosure regarding self-inflicted violence.

Excerpt from *A Rough Couple of Days: Scars*

There's a certain window of time in the middle of the night out in Middle America where there's no bar open and nothing on TV. If you don't want to do too many drugs, you have to start bodily mutilation.

— AniDifranco

What?! What the hell are you talking about, Ani DiFranco?!

I've known many people who have hurt themselves, but it never appeared deliberate — like getting hurt wasn't the primary goal but an unwanted side effect of another activity. Drinking and drugs immediately come to mind. The primary goal of those two activities, as I understand it, is to feel better, not worse. (Although, I think I can count on one fingerless hand the times that I actually felt better after a night of drinking and drugs.)

When Jen told me that she cut herself it sunk in rather slowly, as the information had to pass through layers of misconceptions, the first of which I just mentioned. For me, drugs and alcohol did not fall into the category of self-harm; they were fun — just look at the commercials. How could one miss the tiny clues to this cultural bias? Our language describes one as "partying" and one as "self-mutilation." Since drugs and alcohol were not considered self-harm, I believed that I had no reference point — no experience to draw from to empathize with Jen's experience. It was mysterious and foreign, as if she had told me she was a Muslim suicide bomber. At least those bombers are promised a payoff — an afterlife palace with seventy-two mansions with seventy-two homes with seventy-two sheets on seventy-two beds with seventy-two virgins that never lose their virginity. All sounds quite lovely, really. But cutting? For what? That just seemed crazy.

Yet there she was, on the blue loveseat, looking about five years old, telling me that there was something that she needed to show me — something of which she was very ashamed. Eyes still riveted to the floor, she took in some extra air and asked if I would look at her scars. *God she looked little.* "Okay." She pushed up each sleeve to her elbow, and then drew them both to her chest. Took in a bit more air, closed her eyes, and stretched her arms out in front of her. No more breathing. Head bowed, eyes fixed, waiting for judgment.

I cupped my hands under her elbows and held the weight of her arms. I looked at each scar — alabaster reminders of each time that the pain had gotten so bad that cutting her flesh somehow provided relief. *Oh, my God, how can this happen?! How can this be? How can this poor little girl be so sad? How can this be the solution? How come nobody knows about this? And if people know, how come nobody helped her? How could this make her feel better? Who taught her to communicate with a razor blade?*

Overwhelming sadness. I thought I might lose it, but I swallowed hard, set my jaw, bit the inside of my cheek and looked in her eyes. Fear. I always saw fear. Then she asked me what I was thinking. I couldn't tell her the flood of all that I was thinking. Instead, I told her what I was feeling. "I'm sad, honey. I'm sad that you felt so bad, that you had to do this to yourself. I'm sad and I'm sorry." Her head dropped again. She leaned forward and began to cry. Began to feel her pain instead of managing it. In that moment, she no longer seemed that hard to understand. In fact, it made some sense; she had found something that made her feel better when her emotions threatened to overwhelm her. Not my choice when shopping for a coping mechanism, but it had kept her alive. Kept her alive until she found a way to sit with those feelings — the feelings she believed would kill her.

The razor was the relief, never the threat.

Clinician's Corner: Self-Inflicted Violence

> The truth about childhood is stored up in our body and lives in the depth of our soul. Our intellect can be deceived, our feelings can be numbed and manipulated, our perception shamed and confused, our bodies tricked with medication. But our soul never forgets. And because we are one, one whole soul in one body, someday our body will present its bill.
>
> — Alice Miller

Making the decision to ask Linda to see my scars was scary. And since making the decision to ask was scary, actually doing it was terrifying. I wasn't afraid that she would be repulsed, wasn't afraid that she would judge me — I was afraid she wouldn't see me.

I was so tired of cutting and I was running out of clean skin. It was no longer working as well as it had. I was still in so much pain, so sad, so scared. And so very much alone.

I had tried showing people before. And nothing much changed. Little or no reactions. I know now that maybe they were scared, didn't know what to do, maybe they felt helpless. But because they were professionals, and I was helpless, I needed them to do something.

I couldn't bear the thought of telling someone again — telling Linda — and getting the same response which was nothing.

What I wanted was for her to see me. To see my pain. To see that this was all I could find to help me get through. And I needed her to see my desperation. Needed her to see the sense of urgency. Needed her to get where I was, where I had been and where I wouldn't survive going.

So I sat on the couch and struggled to get the words out. I had told her about my cutting before, so it wouldn't be a total surprise. With my head down — terrified to make eye contact — I asked her if I could show her my scars. What happened next was unbelievable and exactly what I needed. As she said yes, of course, she moved her chair closer to me. Holding her hands out and open, I pulled up my sleeves and rested my forearms, palms up, in her hands. I know I wasn't breathing because as her hands tightened to hold on to me, she reminded me to breathe. And she began to look at my arms, gently tracing her fingers over my scars while remaining present with me and my pain. No words for a while. Just a silent acknowledgement of what was — my attempt to cope, my attempt to tolerate not being seen, my way of surviving abandonment, my way of staying functional in the world — and the horror of what my life had been and subsequently become.

I had never been in this place before. Never sat with someone who was just sad with me. With someone who didn't try to avoid, justify, reduce or change my experience. Just sat with me.

I'm not sure why, but I decided to show her the scars on my torso. They were longer than most — running from one side to past where my belly button indicated my midline. No one had seen these before. These were some of the scars that I struggled with most — especially when I was alone in the shower. Alone with my sadness. Alone.

I didn't go further and show her the scars on my breasts. Or the ones just inside my groin. Or the ones on the back of my legs, on my ankles, on my face. I didn't want to take the risk of pushing her over the edge, of showing too much, or of scaring her away. In this moment, I was being seen. Doing anything that would risk changing that was something I wouldn't, couldn't do. It had been so long. I had been through so much. So many people — family, friends, and professionals — who I had tried to show, yet no one would see. In this moment, nothing was worth the risk of not being seen. And, for the first time, I felt like I just might be able to stop.

CLIENT HANDOUT:
Self-Injury (SI) a.k.a. Self-Inflicted Violence (SIV)

SI and SIV refer to certain forms of violence — cutting, hitting, burning, scratching or punching one's self. The person's intent is not usually to injure or maim his/her body, although it is often a side effect. The violence perpetrated against oneself happens for various reasons. It may be understood as an effective coping mechanism in the management of trauma's sequelae; traumatic abreaction; intense emotion and distress; dissociative symptoms and/or flashbacks. Basically, people use SIV because it helps them manage what feels unbearable in the moment. Although a misconception, SIV is commonly believed to be an attention-seeking manipulation. Although it may be true that their injuries may be upsetting to others, most of the folks who self-injure do so in private — cloaked in secrecy, shrouded in shame.

According to Ruta Mazelis, author of *Demystifying Self-Inflicted Violence: Lessons Learned from the Past Dozen Years, The Cutting Edge*, "Once understood in context, SIV can be healed by acknowledging the needs it serves and addressing the trauma from which it springs. 'People who confront the roots of their pain, and identify the patterns of survival used to manage it, build a relationship with themselves that is based on dignity and self-compassion.'"

The simplest way to explain how to stop the behavior also comes from Mazelis, "People stop living with SIV when they no longer need it, when the reasons they turned to it in the first place are in the process of being healed, and when they expand their options for managing them. Some people focus directly on learning alternatives for SIV and find that useful. Other people never focus directly on managing self-injury and find that it fades away as they work through the trauma issues that brought out the triggers that led to SIV. The common denominator learned from people who have left SIV behind him or her is that each person determined their journey regarding SIV. Coercion from persons or institutions was not effective in helping people stop SIV; in fact, it oftentimes increased not only the SIV, but exacerbated other sequelae of trauma. Force, even if apparently well-intentioned, is most often retraumatizing."

If you are interested in exploring SIV in your life, remember that it is more important for you to focus on understanding it, i.e., what it does for you and how it has or hasn't worked for you — rather than having the focus be immediate cessation of this "problem behavior."

Self-Inflicted Violence, Cont.

Don't turn away keep your gaze on the bandaged place, that's where the light comes in.

— Rumi

Here's the fact: You do this behavior for a reason. Everybody may not understand your reason(s) for the behavior — nor do they need to — but it obviously benefits you in some way. It might get you out of an intensely negative emotional experience; bring you back from a flashback; put you into — or bring you out of — a dissociative episode; communicate emotional distress to others; it may be used as a means of punishment or control; or it may feel like your only alternative to suicide.

Some people have learned self-inflicted violence as a way to manage or control the experience of overwhelm. Other people have had abusive childhood experiences where perpetrators taught them to self-injure rather than remember or disclose the abuse. Self-inflicted violence may be an attempt to integrate some traumatic information or give you a feeling of mastery over your past — a feeling of being in charge and as such, better able to cope with your earlier trauma. You may not even fully understand your reasons for the behavior; you just know that you are less stressed/tense/anxious after the act of self-inflicted violence.

Whatever your reason(s) for the behavior, it makes sense to you. Like all attempts at coping, it was a creative adjustment — in this case, to an earlier dysfunctional environment. It worked for you; it kept you alive. And that's a good thing. A very good thing. If you wish to understand your pattern with this coping mechanism, proceed with the following exercises:

Reasons For Self-Inflicted Violence

- It's soothing and comforting
- It makes me feel powerful
- It stops all my feelings
- Makes me feel alive
- It helps me space out
- It helps me feel grounded
- I need to be punished for being bad/evil
- It makes me feel real
- It helps me forget
- I don't know, I just have to do it
- It just happens
- I feel more in control then
- It's how I show anger
- It helps me cry

- It's how I communicate pain/need
- It's what I know and it works
- It's the only way I can feel sexual
- It relieves tension
- I need to see blood/bruises/insides
- It helps me "go away"
- I can't remember
- I gets me focused
- Nobody can hurt me more than I
- It makes everything less real
- It makes everything more real
- It helps me feel sensation
- It feels right
- It helps me know where I begin/end

SELF-INFLICTED VIOLENCE, CONT.

If other reasons fit better for you, describe them on the lines below:

_____

_____

_____

_____

     Although other people have influence and opinions regarding your behavior, you are ultimately the one who will decide how you will behave. Unless someone places you in five-point leather restraints and sits at your side 24/7, you ultimately have the freedom to act as you will. Although power struggles may ensue, it is virtually impossible to prevent someone from injuring him/herself when that is what (s)he is determined to do.

     It may or may not appear self-evident, but the choice to self-injure is, and will remain, yours (as it should). In fairness, however, you have explored only the benefits of self-inflicted violence. To make an informed decision, you should identify its costs as well. Some people wish that they could stop their self-injuring behavior, citing reasons from shame, isolation, and embarrassment to more concrete reasons like having to wear long sleeves year-round and horrible experiences in the emergency room.

What are some of the costs associated with your use of self-inflicted violence?

_____

_____

_____

_____

     After exploring the costs of self-inflicted violence, you may decide that it is still an effective form of coping; that the benefits outweigh the costs, therefore, decide that now is not the time to give it up. However, after exploring the costs, you may have decided that the costs do in fact outweigh the benefits, so you may wish to try something else. Both choices are valid. No praise; no blame. Keep in mind; it is not uncommon for self-injury to continue alongside self-healing and good therapy.

     If you decide that you want to stop or decrease your use of self-injury, you should remember that behavioral change is slow and recurrences are extremely common. Like everyone else, when stressed, you will tend to revert to old, familiar coping mechanisms, so prepare to start again. Perhaps you might even be gentle with yourself.

If you're going to do this, you're going to need support!

Self-Inflicted Violence, Cont.

Internet Resources for Self-Injury

- One of the biggest and best Self-Harm Support Communities on the Internet:
  http://www.recoveryourlife.com/

- S.A.F.E. Alternatives® (Self-Abuse Finally Ends) is a nationally recognized treatment approach, professional network and educational resource base, which is committed to helping you and others achieve an end to self-injurious behavior:
  http://www.selfinjury.com/

- Formerly Bodies Under Siege SIARI: Self Injury and Related Issues International Internet service of information resources and support:
  http://www.palace.net/~llama/psych/injury.html

- Sidran Institute began collaboration with Ruta Mazelis, the publisher of a newsletter for people living with SIV. Now in its 15th year of publication, this newsletter — The Cutting Edge — serves as a resource for those seeking information on this often-misunderstood issue and includes editorial commentaries, written and artistic contributions from the readership, and reviews of various resources for those who live with SIV. For a PDF version of the most recent issue, go to:
  www.healingselfinjury.org

Self-Inflicted Violence, Cont.

Lots of us have resources that we don't realize we have (friends, family, talents, skills, ideas, etc.). Sometimes it's easier to remember to call upon these resources than at other times. Often identifying and remembering what was helpful in the past gives us ideas about what might be helpful today and in the future.

Have you ever wanted to self-injure and not done it? Once or more than once? When?

_____

_____

_____

What were the circumstances?

_____

_____

_____

What did you do instead?

_____

_____

_____

What made that time (or those times) different from other times you did self-injure?

_____

_____

_____

Are there people who are helpful to be around when you feel like self injuring?

_____

_____

_____

Self–Inflicted Violence, Cont.

Do you have any ideas about what might be helpful (and less costly) when you feel like self-injuring?

_____

_____

_____

Some More Ideas

If you self-injure because it's important to feel pain, you might:

- Hold an ice cube in your hand(s)
- Dunk your face in a bowl/bucket/sink filled with ice water (see client handout "Bobbing for Reality" on page 135)
- Wearing a rubber band on your wrist, snap it
- Using boxing gloves and punching a punching bag
- Splash cold water on your face
- See grounding and centering section for exercises

Can you think of less damaging ways to feel pain?

_____

_____

_____

If you self-injure when remembering difficult or traumatic events you might:

- Do something that feels comforting instead. Explicitly reminding yourself that the abuse or event is not happening now. Although it may feel like it is happening now, the traumatic incident(s) had a beginning, middle and an end. It's over. It's over and you are safe now.

When you have this type of re-experiencing, it may be helpful to:

- Breathe in deeply and slowly.
- Breathe all of the air out.
- Look around.
- Remind yourself who, where and when you are.
- Say to yourself, "Even though I feel scared, it's not happening now. I know that because, I see that picture of me and Kara and this vase that Katie bought for me. . . ." Anything that brings you back to the here and now.
- Remind yourself out loud that you are safe and that these feelings are from a different time.
- Use multisensory imagery to create safe, comfortable places in your imagination where you can go to feel safe.
- Carry around something from the present (a stuffed animal, your therapist's business card, a stone, a photograph of someone you love) to hold on to and look at for comfort.

SELF-INFLICTED VIOLENCE, CONT.

If you self-injure because you can't stop thinking about painful events, are there other ways that you might comfort yourself?

_____

_____

_____

How can you help yourself remember these options the next time you are feeling overwhelmed by these memories?

_____

_____

_____

If you self-injure to help manage your emotions, it's helpful to figure out what the emotion is; why it feels unbearable; then and develop some alternatives to how you might first identify, modulate and decide to express (or not express) the emotion.

Do any of these feelings make you want to self-injure?

Anger	Stupid	Feeling Sexual	Sadness
Loneliness	Fear	Terror	Feeling Small
Shame	Jumpy/Nervous/Anxious	Feeling Cheated	Disappointment
Joy	Annoyance	Aggravation	Less Than
Irritation	Embarrassment	Guilt	Pleasure
	Feeling Used	Vulnerability	

List any other feelings that make you want to self-injure.

_____   _____

_____   _____

_____   _____

Self-Inflicted Violence, Cont.

If emotions are rough for you, it will be useful to work at increasing your tolerance for them — the full spectrum of them. Remember EMOTIONS ARE TRANSIENT! They move through you and, like events, have beginnings, middles and ends. They become problematic for us when we resist or refuse to experience them.

What helps you when you are feeling lost or overwhelmed by feelings?

_____

_____

_____

Do you have ideas about what, besides self-injury, you might try the next time you feel that way?

_____

_____

_____

Sometimes people notice that one feeling leads to another, and then another, until they need to self-injure. Here's an example: feeling sensual pleasure may remind you of abuse, which makes you feel scared, ashamed, and angry. These feelings may cycle so quickly that it is hard to really track what's going on. If this is something that you experience, then you might try:

- Just noticing your pattern.
- Attempt to slow down the process that leads you to self-injure.
- Try noticing each individual emotion, sensation, and thought as they appear.

List them below:

_____

_____

_____

_____

Using the information about your pattern from above, when would be the best time for you to intervene?

_____

_____

_____

SELF-INFLICTED VIOLENCE, CONT.

When might it be too late to intervene?

_____

_____

_____

What interventions might work best at each point?

_____

_____

_____

Since it is often quite difficult to remember these interventions or alternatives in the midst of strong feelings, having a way to remind yourself is quite helpful. How could you remind yourself of these alternatives?

_____

_____

_____

If you self-injure because you need to comfort, self-soothe, or release tension, you may find it helpful to learn some additional methods of achieving internal peace and calmness. Here are some suggestions that others have found helpful.

COMFORT AND SELF-SOOTHING

- Wrapping up tightly in a blanket
- Taking a warm bath or shower
- Yoga poses or meditation
- Rocking yourself — in a chair or just with your body
- Listening to CDs, such as nature sounds, music, or someone's voice that comforts you

RELIEVING TENSION

- Running, jogging, swimming
- Walking or any other form of exercise
- Breaking glass (carefully)
- Stomping on anything (carefully)
- Doing yard work

Self-Inflicted Violence, Cont.

- Throwing things (carefully)
- Pounding pillows or a mattress
- Shredding tissues or paper
- Tearing up phone books

If you use self-injury to self-soothe or release tension, what other things might be helpful for you?

_____

_____

_____

SELF-INJURY CONTRACT

This is my self-injury contract. I've agreed to carry it around with me and refer to if/when I'm upset and want to hurt myself. I won't guarantee that I won't hurt myself, but I guarantee that I'll read and fill it out before I hurt myself.

I want to hurt myself because:

_____

_____

I think it will help me to get through this moment, but it will cost me:

_____

_____

Before I hurt myself, I can:

_____

_____

Four people I can call before I hurt myself:

1. Name : _____ Phone # : _____

2. Name : _____ Phone # : _____

3. Name : _____ Phone # : _____

4. Name : _____ Phone # : _____

One thing that I can try, that has worked before and is almost always comforting to me, is:

_____

_____

The most important reminder for me:

_____

_____

Sign and date: _____

CLINICIAN'S CORNER: AFFECT REGULATION
EMOTIONS, FEELINGS, AND AFFECT

According to neuroscientist, Antonio Damasio, whose research has helped to elucidate the neural basis for the emotions and emotions' central role in social cognition and decision-making, "The mind is built from ideas that are, in one way or another, brain representations of the body." Quoting Spinoza, "the object of the idea constituting the human Mind is the Body." Damasio asserts that the mind is not just embodied; it is about the body. Its function and fundamental nature is to regulate and represent the state of the body (Damasio, 1999). Because clinical research has shown that each are separate phenomena with physiologically distinct processes, Damasio maintains the importance of distinguishing between:

1. Emotions
2. The Feeling of Emotion
3. The Sense of Self, i.e., the known self who is feeling that emotion

1. **Emotions:**
   a. Are largely unlearned body-based, automatic (involuntary) action — programs aimed at the management of life; triggered by brain devices that signal (via expressions or micro-expressions) to others our internal states, i.e., that we are implementing an approach or withdraw system.
   b. Do not cause their bodily symptoms; they are caused by the symptoms. (Remember the James-Lange theory of emotions? It's back.)
   c. Consist of the myriad of small changes to an individual's physiology (e.g., blood pressure, muscle tone, facial appearance) that can be triggered and executed without an individual being aware of it.
   d. Key characteristics of an emotion:
      i. A pattern of complicated collections of chemical and neural responses
      ii. All emotions have some kind of regulatory role, whose function is to assist the organism in maintaining life

    iii. Biologically determined processes depending on innately set brain devices and laid down by long evolutionary history, although expression can be modified by cultural and learning factors

    iv. Located in a very restricted set of sub-cortical brain structures that regulate and represent body states

    v. Emotion brain devices can be engaged automatically

    vi. Following convention, Damasio divides emotion into different types:

        a. The primary (universal) emotions consisting of happiness, sadness, fear, anger, surprise, and disgust

        b. The background emotions such as well-being, malaise, calm, and tension

        c. The secondary (social) emotions such as embarrassment, jealousy, guilt, and pride

  b. Utilize the body as a theatre (using the internal environment, visceral, vestibular and musculo-skeletal systems) and have effects on numerous brain circuits. The collection of these changes becomes the basis for the neural patterns that in turn become the feeling of an emotion.

2. The Feeling of Emotions:

  a. Refers to the generation of a neurological image (image refers to a representative neurological pattern) representing within the human organism that state of emotion. This distinguishes the physicality of the emotion, as a set of bodily changes, and the separate internal representation of that emotion — the feeling.

  b. Composite perceptions of a particular state of the body (actual or simulated), 'A feeling, in essence, is an idea — an idea of the body and, even more particularly, an idea of a certain aspect of the body, its interior, in certain circumstances.'

  c. Composite perceptions of emotion (always perceptions of what was emoted), "A feeling of emotion is an idea of the body when it is perturbed by the emoting process."

  d. A state of altered cognitive resources including learning system changes.

3. The Sense of Self, i.e., the known self who is feeling that emotion:

  a. Requires that the one feeling the emotion has a sense of oneself — a sense of "I-ness." The "I" who is feeling the emotion.

  b. Is essential to affective processes

Affect: is a key part of the process of an organism's interaction with stimuli. The word also refers sometimes to affect display, which is "a facial, vocal, or gestural behavior that serves as an indicator of affect" (APA 2006). Since it's common in the literature, the terms affect and emotion, and hence affect dysregulation and emotion dysregulation, will be used interchangeably.

(EMOTION) AFFECT REGULATION AND DYSREGULATION

Affect regulation refers to implicit and explicit efforts to maximize positive and minimize negative moods and feeling states (Westen, 1985, 1994). The term affect dysregulation (or emotion dysregulation) generally refers to a deficit in the capacity to modulate affect, where emotions tend to spiral out of control; change rapidly; get expressed in their intense, unmodified forms; and/or overwhelm reasoning (Linehan and Heard, 1992; Shedler and Westen, 2004a; Westen, 1991, 1998). Related conceptualizations suggest that clients may also have difficulty recognizing, differentiating, and integrating emotions and emotion-laden representations of the self and significant others (e.g., Kernberg, 1975). This inability to process emotional experience usually results in global, diffuse, undifferentiated affective states that fail to direct the individual to beneficial behavioral or coping responses, but instead, bring forth a range of frantic escape maneuvers, including reckless or self-destructive actions (Krystal, 1974; Linehan and Heard, 1992; Westen, 1991).

Most of the aforementioned — effective in the moment, yet maladaptive and untenable — affect regulation strategies typify efforts to escape emotions that are experienced as overwhelming or intolerable (e.g., Kullgren, 1988; Montgomery, et al., 1989; Yen, et al., 2002). Brown, et al. (2002) identified emotional relief as a primary motivation for suicide attempts. Research findings lend support to models of treatment that underscore the importance of affect regulation. Perhaps the most important aspect of Dialectical Behavior Therapy (Linehan, 1993) is its explicit, well-justified approach to treating deficits in affect regulation. Mentalization-based therapy (Bateman and Fonagy, 2003) addresses the vulnerability to negative affect states and affect dysregulation (e.g., problematic internal working models of self and other that leave the client vulnerable to rejection or feelings of emptiness) and the problematic affect regulation strategies that emerge from chaotic or otherwise traumatic attachment relationships.

WHAT IS MENTALIZING?

- Mentalizing may be defined as perceiving and interpreting behavior as conjoined with intentional mental states.

- Mentalizing is based on assumptions that mental states influence human behavior.

- Mentalizing requires a careful analysis of the circumstances of actions.

- Mentalizing requires a careful analysis of prior patterns of behavior.

- Mentalizing requires an analysis of the experiences the individual has been exposed to.

- Mentalizing, while it demands complex cognitive processes, is mostly preconscious.

- Mental states (e.g., beliefs, unlike most aspects of the physical world) are readily changeable.

- A focus on the products of mentalizing is a more error-prone process than the focus on physical circumstance because it concerns a mere representation of reality rather than reality itself.

- Mentalizing is an imaginative mental activity. (Bateman and Fonagy, 2006)

In addition to Damasio's findings, Cole & Putnam (1992) posit that one's core sense of self is basically defined by their capacity to regulate internal states and the capacity to anticipate and regulate their reaction to stress. Consequently, increasing clients' capacity for emotion regulation becomes a therapeutic priority (van der Kolk, 2001) and prerequisite for working through any traumatic material.

OK. So, how do we do that?

In his work, *Emotions Revealed,* Paul Ekman concluded that here in the West, due to our lack of formal mindfulness training, most of us may be currently incapable of developing impulse awareness, but proposes that an alternative form of consciousness is achievable. He posits that the key to change rests in the development of a specific type of timely awareness concerning why/when we become emotional, for which he coined the term, *attentiveness.* Ekman asserts that if we are to restrain or adjust our emotional behavior at all, then we first need to know if/when we are or are becoming emotional.

> Most people are rarely so attentive to their emotional feelings, but such attentiveness is possible to achieve . . . observe ourselves during an emotional episode, ideally before more than a few seconds have passed. We recognize that we are being emotional and can consider whether or not our response is justified. We can reevaluate, reappraise, and if that is not successful, then direct what we say and do. . . . When that happens, we will feel more in touch, and better able to regulate our emotional life. (Ekman, 2009)

One of the important functions of emotion is to focus our conscious awareness on the present difficulty that is triggering the emotion. If we are to modulate emotional behavior, then we need to develop a distinctive type of emotional consciousness — one that cultivates the capacity to pause and observe our emotional experience in real-time, thereby increasing the gap between impulse and action, thereby granting some degree of behavioral choice in what seems like an automatic response.

This type of emotional consciousness entails more than being cognizant of an emotional state, it is, according to Alan Wallace, "the sense of being aware of what our mind is doing." Unfortunately, in most of our emotional experience we are so much in it, so rapt by the emotion itself that there is no "sense of awareness of what our mind is doing" because there is no part of the mind that is observing, inquiring, or considering our behavior. We may be conscious, but we are certainly not conscious in any sort of a mindful fashion.

Ekman suggests that a comprehensive approach to the development of attentiveness (and for some, even impulse awareness) would include:

1. **Mindfulness Training**

> The very practice of learning to focus attention on an automatic process that requires no conscious monitoring creates the capacity to be attentive to other automatic processes. We breathe without thinking, without conscious direction of each inhalation and exhalation. Nature does not require that we divert our attention to breathing. When we try paying attention to each breath, people find it very hard to do so for more than a minute, if that, without being distracted by thoughts. Learning to focus our attention on breathing takes daily practice, in which we develop new neural pathways that allow us to do it. And here is the punch line: these skills transfer to other automatic processes — benefiting emotional behavior awareness and eventually, in some people, impulse awareness (2007).

Toward developing an understanding of the root causes of emotions the reader is referred to the following section, Emotion Recognition Exercises. For further information, the reader is referred to Ekman, P., *Emotions Revealed: Recognizing Faces and Feelings to Improve Communication and Emotional Life,* 2nd Ed., 2007.

2. Becoming skilled at differentiating between the physiological sensations that accompany each emotion. (Ekman, Levine, Perls and others offer concrete exercises/experiments to increase our awareness of what Gendlin called the "felt sense.") Paying attention to physiological changes and then letting them serve as cues for us to become attentive — giving us the opportunity to consider, reevaluate, or control our emotions. (See sections on Focusing, Somatic Exercises, and Somatic Experiencing.)

3. Since there are times that we regret our emotional behavior, it behooves us to become accustomed to identifying and weakening emotional triggers.

   a. Identify when it is likely that you would become (regrettably) emotional.

   b. Maintain a log/journal of regrettable emotional episodes. Part of becoming more skilled emotion regulation is developing the ability to analyze and understand what has happened once the episode is over, in order to plan for the future.

   c. By anticipating what may occur and knowing your own vulnerabilities, you stand a better chance of preventing the importation of old emotional scripts, thereby reducing the duration of the emotional refractory period.

      i. Tracking these events via written analysis, done shortly after the incident followed by a close examination facilitates identification of not only why these episodes are occurring, but also when they are likely to reoccur and what you can do to prevent them from triggering you in the future.

      ii. Tracking events where you reacted successfully are useful for two reasons. First, one gets to savor an experience of competence and mastery and second, one gets to compare and contrast events that went well to those that caused regret or remorse.

   d. Once you know what the triggers are, you can practice weakening them, thereby cultivating the capacity to choose how you will enact that emotion.

4. Frequently the issue will be what to do once an emotion has begun (and we are in the refractory period, unable to reinterpret what is occurring). If we are being *attentive,* we can try not to intensify the emotion and to inhibit any behavior that would likely escalate the emotional experience. Ekman offers a number of methods for modulating emotional behavior once one is attentive:

   a. Cognitive Reappraisal: a word of caution, "The problem with reappraising is that our refractory period causes us to resist and prevents us from having access to information — stored within us or from the outside — that can disconfirm the emotion. It is much less difficult to reappraise once the refractory period is over." (Ekman 2007)

    b. After the refractory period, you can analyze the situation. Even if your feelings seem justified, you might still choose to interrupt the process and prohibit your actions and speech for a minute to reign in your emotions.

4. Finally, Ekman suggests that by becoming more observant of the emotional states of others with whom we are engaged. Increasing your ability to distinguish the signs of how others are reacting to us emotionally can alert us to be attentive to what it is happening for us. This information may guide us to respond to others' emotions in an appropriate way. (See following section, Emotion Recognition and Mentalization Exercises)

MENTALIZATION AND EMOTION RECOGNITION

The table below is excerpted from Bateman & Fonagy. (The reader is strongly encouraged to review Bateman & Fonagy, 2006 Mentalization-based Treatment for Borderline Personality Disorder: A Practical Guide. In addition, since we've tacitly agreed not to reinvent the wheel, the reader is also strongly encouraged to review Linehan's exquisitely packaged DBT Skills, entitled, Skills Training Manual for Treating Borderline Personality Disorder (1993).)

FYI: MENTALIZING

Mentalizing simply implies a focus on mental states in oneself or in others, particularly in explanations of behavior. That mental states influence behavior is beyond question. Beliefs, wishes, feelings and thoughts whether inside or outside of our awareness, determine what we do. Mentalization is a mostly preconscious imaginative mental activity. It is imaginative because we have to imagine what other people might be thinking or feeling . . . Mentalizing also helps regulate our emotions. Emotions relate directly to our achievement of, or our failure to achieve, specific wishes and desires . . . It is easy to overlook the nonconscious aspect of mentalizing. For something as simple as maintaining a dialogue we need to monitor our conversational partner's state of mind. Perceiving and responding fluidly to their emotions ensures that our conversation goes smoothly. Steimer-Krause and colleagues (1990) demonstrated that we automatically mirror our interlocutors emotional states, adjusting our posture, facial expressions and tone of voice in the process . . . The implicit mentalization of one's own actions is an emotional state (Damasio, 2003) characterized by a sense of oneself as an agent (Marcel, 2003) . . . We have described the simultaneous experience and knowledge of emotion as mentalized affectivity . . . We believe that mentalized affectivity is crucial to the regulation of emotion, that is, without it the capacity to identify, modulate and express one's affects is definitely curtailed (Fonagy *et al.*, 2002) . . . Mentalizing is the key social-cognitive capacity that has allowed human beings to create effective social groups. Mentalizing is acquired in a social context although the predisposition for it must be inherited, just like the propensity for language. As a psychological scientific construct mentalizing is not new and several related constructs help in completing a description of the range of phenomena that the application of the concept in a psychotherapeutic context will entail. Our approach assumes that dysfunctions of mentalization not only create major relationship problems but also lead to subjective distress, which can result in self-harm and suicidality. The close interface between attachment processes and mentalizing is the key to this. Disturbed relationships both undermine and are undermined by failures of mentalization. We therefore argue that the correction of some of these relational malfunctions can be achieved by assisting patients in the recovery of mentalizing (Bateman and Fonagy, 2006).

Emotion Regulation depends on one's ability to recognize, identify and accurately interpret emotions in one's self. Successful relationships depend on one's ability to accurately read, interpret and appropriately respond to other people's emotions. Due to biology, relational misattunement, early neglect and/or abuse, and subsequent trauma, these abilities are generally compromised in folks with Complex PTSD, DESNOS and BPD.

Given the above, it would undoubtedly benefit clients to learn to better (and eventually more quickly) identify their own emotions as well as those of others. What follows are exercises to bring about new awareness. They are based on The James-Lange Theory of Emotion, LeDeux's research and Damasio's work cited above. They have been adapted from Paul Ekman's work, *Emotions Revealed* (2007).

Ekman's research demonstrates that when we produce the facial movements that correspond to a certain emotion, that expression alone triggers the exact changes in physiology as that of a spontaneous emotion in the body and brain. The idea of practicing the exercises below is to become familiar with emotions — their internal and external environmental signals.

CLIENT HANDOUT:
EMOTION RECOGNITION: SADNESS

Ekman's research demonstrates that producing the emotions' corresponding facial movements, trigger changes in physiology in the body and brain. The idea is to become familiar with emotions and their external environmental signals. By becoming familiar with these emotions and reflecting on what they feel like, you will have a better chance of recognizing them earlier before they become unbearable.

However, the unpleasant (possibly painful) feelings and sensations that you may feel with this exercise on sadness should be noted. Some common reactions during sadness are heavy eyelids; rising cheeks; tightening sensation or a lump in the throat; watery eyes. People differ in how they experience sadness, knowing your own process and how it may differ from those you care about may help you better understand some of the miscommunications and misinterpretations that may occur or may have occurred in your life.

Instructions: You will be watching your reflection in a mirror, as you replicate the facial movements that accompany the primary emotions of sadness, anger and fear. Once you begin to "feel" the emotion, if bearable, let it expand.

Caution: Experiencing the facial muscle movement exercises, most people will experience some sadness, but if the feeling grows extremely strong or is held for long, it might change to anguish. Know what is manageable for you and stop if you become overwhelmed at any time.

Replicating the facial movements of sadness:

1. Drop your mouth open.
2. Pull the corners of your lips down.
3. While holding the lip corners down, aim to raise your cheeks, like you are squinting (so it pulls against the lip corners).
4. Keep the tension between the raised cheeks and the lip corners pulling down.
5. Allow your eyes to glance downward and your upper eyelids to sag and droop.
   a. Although a bit more difficult, try to:
      i. Pull your eye brows together and up in the middle only, drawing the inner corners of your eyebrows up in the middle only, not the entire brow.
      ii. Continue looking downward as your upper eyelids sag and droop.

EMOTION RECOGNITION: SADNESS, CONT.

If you were able to safely experience sadness, try repeating it, before answering the following questions. Concentrate on what those facial movements feel like, paying particular attention to your own process as you first begin to experience the feelings:

1. How does the feeling register?

2. How does it change your awareness and perception of your internal environment?

3. How does it change your awareness and perception of your external environment?

4. What changes do you notice in your:

Head: _____

Neck: _____

Face: _____

Throat: _____

Area in your chest surrounding your heart: _____

Shoulders: _____

Upper back: _____

Lower back: _____

Arms: _____

Stomach: _____

Legs: _____

5. As you let the feeling expand, what sensations or changes in sensations do notice in your:

Head: _____

Neck: _____

Face: _____

Throat: _____

Area in your chest surrounding your heart: _____

Shoulders: _____

Upper back: _____

Lower back: _____

Arms: _____

Stomach: _____

Legs: _____

CLIENT HANDOUT:
EMOTION RECOGNITION: ANGER

Ekman's research demonstrates that producing the emotions' corresponding facial movements triggers changes in physiology in the body and brain. The idea is to become familiar with emotions and their external environmental signals. People differ in how they experience anger, knowing your own process and how it may differ from those you care about may help you better understand some of the miscommunications and misinterpretations that may occur or may have occurred in your life.

Angry sensations include feelings of strain, pressure, and heat. You may feel your heart and respiratory rate increase. As your blood pressure rises, you may feel and see your face redden. Notice your inclination to bite down hard, upper against lower teeth, and to push your chin forward. You may also notice an impulse to move forward. These are the sensations that most people feel.

Caution: Experiencing the facial muscle movement exercises, most people will experience anger. Know how much anger is manageable for you and stop if you become overwhelmed at any time.

Instructions: You will be watching your reflection in a mirror, as you replicate the facial movements that accompany the primary emotion of anger. Once you begin to "feel" the emotion, if bearable, let it expand. After thirty seconds or so have passed, relax and consider what you felt.

Replicating the facial movements of anger:

1. Pull your eyebrows down and together: make certain that the inner corners go down toward your nose.

2. While holding your eyebrows down, attempt to open your eyes real wide (your upper eyelids are pushing against your lowered eyebrows.)

3. Stare intensely.

4. Once you are certain that you are making the correct eyebrow and eyelid movements, relax the upper part of your face.

5. Concentrating on the lower part of your face, begin to press your lips together tightly and tense up both your lips; don't pucker, just press the lips together.

6. Once you are certain that you are making the correct lower-face movements, add in the upper face, lowering your eyebrows, pulling them together, and raising your upper eyelids to stare intensely.

EMOTION RECOGNITION: ANGER, CONT.

If you were able to safely experience anger, try repeating it before answering the following questions. Concentrate on what those facial movements feel like, paying particular attention to your own process as you first begin to experience the feelings:

1. How does the feeling register?

2. How does it change your awareness and perception of your internal environment?

3. How does it change your awareness and perception of your external environment?

4. What changes do you notice in your body?

   Head: _____

   Neck: _____

   Face: _____

   Throat: _____

   Area in your chest surrounding your heart: _____

   Shoulders: _____

   Upper back: _____

   Lower back: _____

   Arms: _____

   Stomach: _____

   Legs: _____

5. As you let the feeling expand, what sensations or changes in sensations do notice in your:

   Head: _____

   Neck: _____

   Face: _____

   Throat: _____

   Area in your chest surrounding your heart: _____

   Shoulders: _____

   Upper back: _____

   Lower back: _____

   Arms: _____

   Stomach: _____

   Legs: _____

CLIENT HANDOUT:
EMOTION RECOGNITION: FEAR

Ekman's research demonstrates that producing the emotions' corresponding facial movements, trigger changes in physiology in the body and brain. The idea is to become familiar with emotions and their external environmental signals. People differ in how they experience fear, you may find that your hands get colder; that you're breathing more quickly and/or deeply; that you may begin to perspire; you may feel trembling or tightening of your large muscles; you may feel your face or body beginning to retreat into the chair. People almost always recognize when they are terrified, but many of us are not as familiar with the sensations that accompany slighter variations of fear. Knowing your own process and how it may differ from those you care about may help you better understand some of the miscommunications and misinterpretations that may occur or may have occurred in your life.

Caution: Experiencing the facial muscle movement exercises, most people will experience fear. Know how much fear is manageable for you and stop if you become overwhelmed at any time.

Instructions: You will be watching your reflection in a mirror, as you replicate the facial movements that accompany the primary emotion, fear. Once you begin to "feel" the emotion, if bearable, let it expand. After thirty seconds or so have passed, relax and consider what you felt.

Replicating the facial movements of fear:

1. Raise your upper eyelids as high as possible.

2. If possible, slightly tense your lower eyelids (if tensing your lower eyelids interferes with raising your upper eyelids, and then just focus on raising your upper eyelids.)

3. Let your jaw go slack.

4. With your jaw dropped, stretch you lips horizontally back toward your ears. (If this is not possible, then just let your jaw hang open.)

5. With your upper eyelids raised as high as they can go, stare intensely straight ahead.

6. Raise your eyebrows as high as you can.

7. With brows raised, pull your eyebrows together (if you can't do both, then just keep the eyebrows raised with your upper eyelids raised).

You may find that your hands get colder; that you're breathing more quickly and/or deeply; that you may begin to perspire; you may feel trembling or tightening of your large muscles; you may feel your face or body beginning to retreat into the chair. People usually recognize when they are terrified, but may not be as familiar with the sensations that accompany slighter variations of fear.

EMOTION RECOGNITION: FEAR, CONT.

Concentrate on what those facial movements feel like — paying particular attention to your own process as you first begin to experience the feelings:

1. How does the feeling register?

2. What is your breathing like?

3. Do you notice a change in temperature?

4. How does it change your awareness and perception of your internal environment?

5. How does it change your awareness and perception of your external environment?

6. What other changes do you notice in your body?

Head: _____

Neck: _____

Face: _____

Throat: _____

Area in your chest surrounding your heart: _____

Shoulders: _____

Upper back: _____

Lower back: _____

Arms: _____

Stomach: _____

Legs: _____

7. As you let the feeling expand, what sensations or changes in sensations do you notice in your:

Head: _____

Neck: _____

Face: _____

Throat: _____

Area in your chest surrounding your heart: _____

Shoulders: _____

Upper back: _____

Lower back: _____

Arms: _____

Stomach: _____

Legs: _____

CLINICIAN'S CORNER:
PATHOLOGICAL DISSOCIATION

The International Society for the Study of Trauma and Dissociation (ISSTD) posts on its website:

> Dissociation is a word that is used to describe the disconnection or lack of connection between things usually associated with each other. Dissociated experiences are not integrated into the usual sense of self, resulting in discontinuities in conscious awareness (Anderson & Alexander, 1996; Frey, 2001; International Society for the Study of Dissociation, 2002; Maldonado, Butler, & Spiegel, 2002; Pascuzzi & Weber, 1997; Rauschenberger & Lynn, 1995; Simeon, *et al.*, 2001; Spiegel & Cardeña, 1991; Steinberg, *et al.*, 1990, 1993). In severe forms of dissociation, disconnection occurs in the usually integrated functions of consciousness, memory, identity, or perception. For example, someone may think about an event that was tremendously upsetting yet have no feelings about it. Clinically, this is termed emotional numbing, one of the hallmarks of post-traumatic stress disorder. Dissociation is a psychological process commonly found in persons seeking mental health treatment (Maldonado, *et al.,* 2002) . . . Research tends to show that dissociation stems from a combination of environmental and biological factors . . . Most commonly, repetitive childhood physical and/or sexual abuse and other forms of trauma are associated with the development of dissociative disorders (e.g., Putnam, 1985). In the context of chronic, severe childhood trauma, dissociation can be considered adaptive because it reduces the overwhelming distress created by trauma. However, if dissociation continues to be used in adulthood, when the original danger no longer exists, it can be maladaptive. The dissociative adult may automatically disconnect from situations that are perceived as dangerous or threatening, without taking time to determine whether there is any real danger. This leaves the person "spaced out" in many situations in ordinary life, and unable to protect themselves in conditions of real danger. . . There are five main ways in which the dissociation of psychological processes changes the way a person experiences living: depersonalization, derealization, amnesia, identity confusion, and identity alteration. These are the main areas of investigation in the Structured Clinical Interview for Dissociative Disorders (SCID-D) (Steinberg, 1994a; Steinberg, Rounsaville, & Cicchetti, 1990). A dissociative disorder is suggested by the robust presence of any of the five features.

For further information visit: http://www.isst-d.org/

In an article entitled, "The Dissociative Capsule," Scaer explains traumatic dissociation with such clarity that I requested that he let me reprint it. Not only because I wanted to get out of that writing assignment, but also because I have never seen it elucidated so well. The most gracious of gurus, he granted not only permission, but also blessing and encouragement. Thanks! *(For the full article visit his website: www.traumasoma.com)*

Scaer writes:

Dissociation, almost by definition, is characterized by a unique and rather sharply defined state of altered perception that is different from reality. As a *state*, we can assign it quite specific features, based on its unique alteration in various types of perception, all of which are memories for past experiences. As a specific state, it will be defined by the boundaries of its content, and I would therefore like to present the metaphorical, but quite functional definition of the *dissociative capsule*. The content of a specific capsule will consist of procedural memories for the autonomic, *somatosensory* and *emotional feelings* of the trauma. All of these states of course are associated with body sensations. Autonomic states (fight/flight/freeze) are associated with cardiac and visceral feelings — pounding heart, cold hands, tremor, chest pressure, gut tightness and cramps. Emotions also are associated with feelings such as the tingling rush of joy, the heavy sinking feeling of depression, the face — burning, constricting feeling of shame. And somatosensory sensations (from the muscles, skin and skeleton) contribute to all of these feelings — tightening of neck and back muscles, tingling of the skin, pressure in the head, even severe pain. Of course, this capsule would also contain the very specific emotion-linked conscious memories of the event as well. And finally, since endorphins were released in large amounts at the time of the threat and the freeze response that initiated the traumatic event, perceptions of the dissociative capsule will often be distorted and bizarre.

The dissociative capsule would be quite specific to the traumatic event that defined it, and would consist of the sum total of all of those procedural memories reflecting the experiences of the event that were stored, in their finest detail in a diverse grouped cluster of perceptions. These diverse procedural memories, hard-wired and permanent, would be susceptible to recall in the face of both internal and external environmental cues that reflect elements of the traumatic event . . . That recall by definition would occur in the course of some present moment, and would be perceived as *being present*, even though it reflected a past moment. It would interrupt the present moment for a variable period of time depending on the intensity and specificity of the cues. It could last a few seconds, or in the case of numerous large capsules, could occupy one's present moment most or all of the time. Emergence of the dissociative capsule into the present moment would destroy its function (intentionality, acquisition of new memory and evolution of the sense of self). The present moment would consist of old emotionally-based declarative memories and feelings from the body reflecting the autonomic, emotional and somatic input from traumatic procedural memory. During this obliteration of the present moment, the person would exist in the past traumatic experience, would respond to its messages as if confronted with the old trauma, and would be unable to form plans of action or store new memories based on current experience. For that brief or prolonged period of time, consciousness and the mind would be rendered inert. The victim would be frozen in a past traumatic moment, and their perception would reflect that moment. Finally, the inevitable release of endorphins with emergence of the dissociative capsule would cloud cognition and perception, creating the surreal state of dissociative perception.

Robert C. Scaer, MD, website: www.traumasoma.com

- *The Body Bears the Burden: Trauma, Dissociation and Disease.* Haworth Press. (2007).

- *The Trauma Spectrum: Hidden Wounds and Human Healing.* W.W. Norton and Co. (2005).

On Daniel Baldwin's *Trauma Pages*, Nijenhuis writes,

Many traumatized individuals alternate between re-experiencing their trauma and being detached from, or even relatively unaware of the trauma and its effects (APA, 1994; Nijenhuis & Van der Hart, 1999). This alternating pattern has been noted for more than a century by students of psychotraumatology (Janet, 1889, 1904; Kardiner, 1941; Horowitz, 1976), who have observed that it can ensue after different degrees and kinds of traumatization. It is characteristic of post-traumatic stress disorder (PTSD; APA, 1994), disorder of extreme stress (DES; Pelcovitz *et al.*, 1997), and many cases of trauma-related dissociative disorders (Nijenhuis & Van der Hart, 1999). With delayed PTSD, the pattern starts after an extended period of relatively well functioning. A few traumatized individuals develop dissociative amnesia as a disorder which involves reported gaps in recall related to the trauma, additional aspects of their prior life, or even all of it (Markowitsch, 1999; Van der Hart, Brown, & Graafland, 1999; Van der Hart & Nijenhuis, 2001). These patients remain amnesic for an extended period of time. Eventual retrieval of the trauma can resolve the disorder, but in some cases a pattern of alternation between amnesia and re-experience of trauma develops (for a review, see Van der Hart, *et al.,* 2000). The theory also suggests a host of treatment guidelines (see below) that cannot be elaborated here (see Steele, Van der Hart, & Nijenhuis, in press). Briefly, it indicates that the treatment of trauma-related disorders, including DID, involves integration of feared mental contents in ways that are adapted to the current integrative capacity of the patient. The treatment basically concerns resolution of the structural dissociation of the personality by exposing the dissociative parts of the personality, and their mental contents, to each other in carefully planned steps that promote integration and preclude re-dissociation.

> Nijenhuis, E.R.S.; Van der Hart, O. & Steele, K. (2004). "Trauma-related structural dissociation of the personality." *Trauma Information Pages* website, January 2004.

For further information visit: http://www.trauma-pages.com/a/nijenhuis-2004.php

To obtain treatment guidelines (they're free!)

GUIDELINES FOR TREATING DISSOCIATIVE IDENTITY DISORDER IN ADULTS.

TO OBTAIN ASSESSMENT MATERIALS

Website: www.isst-d.org/education/Adult%20DD%20Treatment%20Guidelines-ISSTD-JTD-2005.pdf

GUIDELINES FOR THE EVALUATION AND TREATMENT OF DISSOCIATIVE SYMPTOMS IN CHILDREN AND ADOLESCENTS

TO OBTAIN ASSESSMENT MATERIALS

Website: www.isst-d.org/education/ChildGuidelines-ISSTD-2003.pdf

THE DISSOCIATIVE EXPERIENCES SCALE, II

The DES is a brief, self-report measure of the frequency of dissociative experiences. The scale was developed to provide a reliable, valid, and convenient way to quantify dissociative experiences. The Dissociative Experiences Scale (DES) was developed by Eve Bernstein Carlson, Ph.D., and Frank W. Putnam, M.D., The overall DES score is obtained by adding up the 28 item scores and dividing by 28: this yields an overall score ranging from 0 to 100. DES is not a diagnostic instrument; it is a screening instrument. Copies of the DES and the A-DES are copyright-free. You are welcome to photocopy any of the materials for use in research or clinical work. You do not need special permission to use the DES in your research or clinical work. Copies of the DES are packaged with reprints of the article, *An Update on the Dissociative Experiences Scale* (Dissociation 6 (1):16–27), which is a manual for the DES, and a list of 333 references for studies that have used or discussed the use of the DES as a measure of dissociation.

Eve Bernstein Carlson, Ph.D. & Frank W. Putnam, M.D.
Mean DES Scores Across Populations for Various Studies

General Adult Population	5.4
Anxiety Disorders	7.0
Affective Disorders	9.3
Eating Disorders	15.8
Late Adolescence	16.6
Schizophrenia	15.4
Borderline Personality Disorder	19.2
PTSD	31
Dissociative Disorder (NOS)	36
Dissociative Identity Disorder (MPD)	48

The DES II measures three main factors of Dissociation:

Amnesia Factor: This factor measures memory loss, i.e., not knowing how you got somewhere, being dressed in clothes you don't remember putting on, finding new things among belongings you don't remember buying, not recognizing friends or family members, finding evidence of having done things you don't remember doing, finding writings, drawings or notes you must have done, but don't remember doing.

Depersonalization/Derealization Factor: Depersonalization is characterized by the recurrent experience of feeling detached from one's self and mental processes or a sense of unreality of the self. Items relating to this factor include feeling that you are standing next to yourself or watching yourself do something and seeing yourself as if you were looking at another person, feeling your body does not belong to you, and looking in a mirror and not recognizing yourself. Derealization is the sense of a loss of reality of the immediate environment. These items include feeling that other people, objects, and the world around them is not real, hearing voices inside your head that tell you to do things or comment on things you are doing, and feeling like you are looking at the world through a fog, so that people and objects appear far away or unclear.

Absorption Factor: This factor includes being so preoccupied or absorbed by something that you are distracted from what is going on around you. The absorption primarily has to do with one's traumatic experiences. Items of this factor include realizing that you did not hear part or all of what was said by another, remembering a past event so vividly that you feel as if you are reliving the event, not being sure whether things that you remember happening really did happen or whether you just dreamed them, when you are watching television or a movie you become so absorbed in the story you are unaware of other events happening around you, becoming so involved in a fantasy or daydream that it feels as though it were really happening to you, and sometimes sitting, staring off into space, thinking of nothing, and being unaware of the passage of time.

To Obtain Assessment Materials:

    Website: www.sidran.org

CLIENT HANDOUT:
DISSOCIATION: YOU'RE GROUNDED!

"Why would I want to be here; it sucks here!"
"It's scary here!"
" I hate being in my body! I prefer to be in my own little world!"

OK, but just a few questions before you leave . . .

- Is this strategy still helpful?

- Does it keep you safe? Does it let you live your life fully? What are the associated costs?

- Is it actually dangerous in the here and now?

- Did you know that use of dissociation to cope with present stressors usually brings up the same thoughts, feelings and body sensations that you had in the past, making it hard to know that things are different today?

- Do you have skills to deal with *scared body*?

- Did you know that dissociation and numbing necessarily obstruct problem-solving in the present?

- Did you know that staying focused on the past or spinning fearful future scenarios, you may not be able to tell the difference between what you are feeling and what is really happening?

- Did you know that when you use this coping strategy, you might not be able to remember that things are different now, e.g., that you have support and new resources?

- Did you know that shutting things out increases the traumatic stress responses you will have later?

- Did you know that dissociation keeps you emotionally trapped in the past; prevents emotional growth; and makes it nearly impossible to develop healthy relationships?

How do I know if I'm not grounded? How do I recognize the stress responses?

Dissociation: You're Grounded, Cont.

The Signs and Symptoms

- Purposeful dissociation and/or spontaneous trance may feel like you are disappearing (like you are checking out, zoning out, or like you've been drugged); depersonalizing (like you aren't real); or derealization (like the world isn't real).

- Switching may feel like something or someone else is taking over, like you are slipping away, or like some other part inside is in control now. Losing time — it may seem that there is a gap in what just happened or that you are filling in the blanks, or coming back in the middle of something.

- Age regression may make you feel as if you are getting smaller or feeling younger; like everything else is getting bigger; your clothes or your skin don't seem to fit; your hands may seem to be getting bigger; you may feel helpless, frozen, and unable to talk.

- Hypervigilance feels like being on guard, needing to keep track of everything going on around you, jumping at every sound, or watching for the threat that you feel is there. It makes you feel as if you are threatened, although you aren't.

- Numbing may make you feel like you are separated from your body, or as if you have no body and/or no feelings.

- Avoidance gets you away from something that feels overwhelming.

- Flashbacks may make you feel like you are experiencing some part of the trauma again. Initially, it is common to experience flashbacks as intense emotions, body sensations, or physical pains that are not connected to anything in the present. You may see or hear things related to trauma even though they aren't happening NOW.

Grounding and centering increases your awareness of what is actually going on presently — internally and externally. It involves skills that will keep you oriented times three. (In laymen terms, it will help you remember a few key truths):

1. Who you are — an adult in an adult body (person)
2. Where you are — location in the present (place)
3. When you are — the present day and date (time)

Answering these questions and connecting with the truth of those answers, will decrease the likelihood of your losing track of the differences between the past and the present, making it less likely that you'll experience the distress caused by the flashbacks and dissociative experiences. It is important to be able to focus on present reality no matter how you are feeling or what part of yourself is in control. In this way, you will be grounded throughout the range of emotions, moods, and identity states.

GROUNDING AND CENTERING EXERCISES

USING YOUR FIVE SENSES

- **Sight:** Lights on! Eyes open! Now, look around; identify, label, and describe what you see all around you, e.g., this picture is of my three nieces at Jimmy's party. Connect with the present, e.g., my sister's kids are big now, so I am an adult. That's my coat, size 10 long- an adult size coat.

- **Sound:** Listen up! Identify and label the sounds around you — sing, read aloud, pray, or listen to the comforting sound of your own adult voice.

- **Taste:** Suck on a mint; chew some peppermint gum; chew on a basil leaf; drink *grapefruit juice* (unless you're taking Wellbutrin), herbal tea, or coffee; use tastes that connect you with being not only safe, but also grown-up.

- **Smell:** Use scented hand lotion, body oil, a loved-one's perfume or aftershave on a piece of cloth or cotton ball, or scented candles, essential oils, or potpourri — anything that reminds you of the present.

- **Touch:** Find a transition object to keep with you at all times — rocks, medals, piece of cloth, or a blanket. Try to get one from a loved one or a support person to keep the connection to that person a bit more concrete. Feel the object's texture, bringing you back to the present. Animals are ideal for this sensory pleasure; pet a cat or dog connecting with its vital, loving presence connecting you back to the here and now.

GROUNDING AND CENTERING (SENSORY SUGGESTIONS)

Sight	Sound	Taste	Smell	Touch
Clock/Calendar	Soothing music	Altoids	Essential oils	Scented body lotion
Photographs (nature, family, friends, inspiration)	Nature sounds	Drop of clove oil or flavored toothpicks	Incense, Vick's Vapo-Rub, anything mentholated	A smooth/textured stone
Look outside, notice just what is there	Familiar sounds (save supportive voice mails, call and listen to a loved one's voicemail)	Grapefruit juiced (unless taking Wellbutrin)	Body lotion/ perfume	Ice cube
TV	Sing, read, or pray; Read/sing aloud	Basil or peppermint leaf	Clove/cinnamon, lemon	Blanket/cloth

THE RELIEF PROJECT

One type of response to traumatic experiences is avoidance of sensory stimuli (scents, tastes, sights, sounds, and textures) associated with the trauma. This reaction effectively limits painful sensory stimuli, but consequently deprives you of all sensory pleasure as well. Choosing to provide yourself with some positive sensory experiences can be not only enjoyable, but empowering. Visiting an arboretum or garden to smell the flowers, going to a petting zoo or a fabric store to touch something soft, enjoying the taste of a piece of ripe fruit, and listening to music are some examples of self-soothing activities that are directly linked to the senses. Because it isn't always possible to soothe yourself through actual life experiences, sometimes it is more convenient to use your imagination. You can use pictures to invoke imaginary sensations that help you shift from a state of distress to one of relative calm. In this way, you can provide yourself with a relaxing break during stressful or unpleasant periods.

In this art experience, you will compile a "relief book" of images to reduce distress by helping you to conjure up positive sensory experiences.

Time: The Relief Project will take about an hour.

Materials: a sketchbook or a copybook, some magazines, scissors and glue.

1. Make a list of experiences in each of the five senses that are (or have been in the past) pleasant for you, e.g., what is your favorite perfume? Comfort foods? Silk, satin or fleece? Waves? Classical music, a loved one's voice? Paintings, photos, sunsets?

Sights:

_____

_____

Sounds:

_____

_____

Tastes:

_____

_____

Scents:

_____

_____

Textures:

_____

_____

2. Look through magazines and cut out pictures of things that are soothing and/or enjoyable to you.

3. Glue each picture onto a separate page or make five separate collages for each of your senses.

4. Personalize your sketchbook/copybook cover in whatever style appeals.

5. Write about your process in your copybook

   a. First, describe any sensations, thoughts, and/or feelings you experienced while selecting the pictures for your book.

   b. For which of your sense(s) did you collect the most pictures? If you favored one or two over the rest, you may want to find ways to increase your actual exposure to those pleasant sensory experiences.

   c. Look through the book and choose one picture that is particularly soothing or pleasing. Spend a minute focusing on it. Then, if you are comfortable closing your eyes, do so and permit yourself to enter into the picture. Be in the experience allowing it to become as vivid as possible.

   d. Did anything surprise you during the exercise, the imagery or the reflection?

   e. When might you benefit from looking through your virtual sensory vacation?

   f. List some circumstances when you might experience some relief from using the book.

6. Recall and list three feelings or thoughts that let you know that you aren't grounded (e.g., staring off, feeling unreal or disconnected; hands appearing bigger; things getting smaller; voices sounding garbled or muffled).

_____

_____

_____

7. Recall and list three situations in the past two weeks where you knew that you were not grounded.

_____

_____

_____

8. Recall and list three situations in the past two weeks where you knew that you were grounded.

_____

_____

_____

9. Now, identify things that help you feel grounded (e.g., petting my dog keeps me present; I'm usually grounded at my desk at work).

_____

_____

_____

10. List some reasons why you think being grounded would be threatening (e.g., feelings are too much; I can't deal with being here).

_____

_____

_____

11. Do any of the reasons apply to your past? Do they still apply in the present, or are they for another time?

_____

_____

_____

DISSOCIATION: YOU'RE GROUNDED, CONT.

Since getting grounded in the present may be unfamiliar, consider that some things are helpful; others not so much:

Helpful	Not so Helpful
Look around (what's really here in the present?)	Ruminating on or entertaining scary thoughts: anything that increases your fear, helplessness, hopelessness, or anxiety will increase the urge to dissociate
Breathe deeply	
Move around	Identify and avoid any repetitive behaviors like rocking, staring, humming, or anything else you have done in the past to "check out, go away," or dissociate.
Feel your arms and legs (rub or lightly massage)	
Say comforting, affirming things to yourself	
Remind yourself of safe and positive people, places, or things	

GROUNDING EXERCISE FOR DISSOCIATION
FIVE COUNTDOWN

This is an exercise to practice staying present.

Count out five things you can touch. Get up and touch each one as you name it and count it off. Come back and write each one down.

1. _____
2. _____
3. _____
4. _____
5. _____

Count out five things you can see. Look at each one as you name it and write it down.

1. _____
2. _____
3. _____
4. _____
5. _____

Count out five things you can hear. Listen to each one as you name it, write it, and count it off.

1. _____
2. _____
3. _____
4. _____
5. _____

Count out five things you can taste or smell. Taste/smell each one as you name it, write it and count it off.

1. _____
2. _____
3. _____
4. _____
5. _____

DISSOCIATION: YOU'RE GROUNDED, CONT.

Now . . .
Count off four things you can touch. Touch each one as you name it, write it, and count it off.

    1. _____

    2. _____

    3. _____

    4. _____

Count off four things you can see. Look at each one as you name it, write it, and count it off.

    1. _____

    2. _____

    3. _____

    4. _____

Count off four things you can hear. Listen to each one as you name it, write it, and count it off.

    1. _____

    2. _____

    3. _____

    4. _____

Count off four things you can taste or smell. Taste/smell each one as you name it, write it, and count it off.

    1. _____

    2. _____

    3. _____

    4. _____

Now. . .
Count off three things you can touch. Touch each one as you name it, write it, and count it off.

    1. _____

    2. _____

    3. _____

Count off three things you can see. Look at each one as you name it, write it, and count it off.

    1. _____

    2. _____

    3. _____

DISSOCIATION: YOU'RE GROUNDED, CONT.

Count off three things you can hear. Listen to each one as you name it, write it, and count it off.

1. _____
2. _____
3. _____

Count off three things you can taste or smell. Taste/smell each one as you name it, write it, and count it off.

1. _____
2. _____
3. _____

Now. . .
Count off two things you can touch. Touch each one as you name it, write it, and count it off.

1. _____
2. _____

Count off two things you can see. Look at each one as you name it, write it, and count it off.

1. _____
2. _____

Count off two things you can hear. Listen to each one as you name it, write it, and count it off.

1. _____
2. _____

Count off two things you can taste or smell. Taste/smell each one as you name it, write it, and count it off.

1. _____
2. _____

Now. . .
Count off one thing you can touch. Touch it as you name it, write it, and count it off.

1. _____

Count off one thing you can see. Look at it as you name it, write it, and count it off.

1. _____

Count off one thing you can hear. Listen to it as you name it, write it, and count it off.

1. _____

Count off one thing you can taste or smell. Taste/smell it as you name it, write it down, and count it off.

1. _____

GROUNDING AND CENTERING
FLASHBACKS

Flashbacks are those intrusive experiences that feel as if they are happening in the present, BUT really aren't. They are compelling; it's as if we were seeing, hearing, and feeling the experience in the present, but in reality, it occurred in the past. These intrusions are triggered episodic memories that have yet to be processed and integrated into our long-term memory.

Because they feel so compelling, it becomes essential to remind oneself that it's not happening now; that it's old stuff. Most people have found it helpful to stay grounded, with one foot always in the present, even when the distressing memory intrudes.

Can you think of some helpful things to remind yourself that it isn't happening now? What would ground you and decrease the fear that accompanies these experiences?

_____

_____

_____

_____

_____

_____

_____

SUGGESTIONS

- It's not happening now.

- Even though my body feels scared, I'm safe now.

- This is a symptom, a traumatic stress reaction.

- What is this experience telling me?

- Is there something that I could be doing that I might like?

Identify three goals related to grounding that you can work on practicing this week:

1. _____

2. _____

3. _____

GROUNDING AND CENTERING

DISSOCIATION LOG

Use this log to keep track of how grounded, centered, and focused you are this week. Put a number from 1 to 10 in each box, for each hour of each day, denoting your level of groundedness for that hour.

Grounded   **Not Grounded**

| 1 | 2 | 3 | 4 | 5 | 6 | 7 | 8 | 9 | 10 |

		Monday	Tuesday	Wednesday	Thursday	Friday	Saturday
8:00 a.m.							
9:00 a.m.							
10:00 a.m.							
11:00 a.m.							
12:00 p.m.							
1:00 p.m.							
2:00 p.m.							
3:00 p.m.							
4:00 p.m.							
5:00 p.m.							
6:00 p.m.							
7:00 p.m.							
8:00 p.m.							
9:00 p.m.							
10:00 p.m.							

DISSOCIATION: YOU'RE GROUNDED, CONT.

GROUNDING AND CENTERING
DISSOCIATION LOG (PART 2)

1. Do you notice any patterns?

   _____

   _____

   _____

2. Do they mean anything to you?

   _____

   _____

   _____

3. Are certain days or certain times of the day particularly difficult to stay present?

   _____

   _____

   _____

4. Pay attention to triggers in the environment. What happens just before you dissociate, "go away," or check out?

   _____

   _____

   _____

5. Are they related to past trauma?

   _____

   _____

   _____

YOU'RE GROUNDED!
PROTECTIVE CONTAINER EXERCISE

People who have experienced trauma often become engulfed or overwhelmed by thoughts and feelings. Sometimes these thoughts and feelings lead to non-adaptive, even harmful behavior. If this is true for you, this containment exercise may help. Containment images and techniques improve your global functioning and sense of well-being. These images will help you to store or put away distressing or overwhelming images, memories, or feelings for exploration at a more convenient time, i.e., like when you are not at work/school or any other place where you are expected to be present, focused, and functioning. Containment does not mean avoidance; it means postponement. You postpone attending to traumatic material until you are adequately supported. In this exercise, you will create an image of a container that will hold any/all intrusive material until the proper time for reprocessing. Containment will provide you with a method of self-control that can protect you from being further traumatized. Once you are well-supported and emotionally stabilized, you will determine when and how to explore these thoughts, memories, feelings, and impulses. By taking them out one by one, you titrate the experience, increasing your tolerance to them.

This exercise will allow you to create an image of a container to temporarily store intrusive thoughts and overwhelming feelings. It will take about an hour. You will need: Drawing paper, colored pencils, or acrylic/water paints (brushes, palette, and water)

1. Identify one overwhelming feeling, intrusive thought, or unhealthy impulse that you would like to temporarily contain.

2. Think about what this container would need to contain these. What features would be necessary if it were designed properly to safely hold this thought, feeling, or impulsive behavior? It can be simple, elaborate, big, or small. The more ownership you take in the container and the more personalized it is the more effective it will be. The following describes some containers and their characteristic features:

   • A chained trunk located under the ocean, to confine traumatic flashbacks.

   • A locked room located at the end of a long castle corridor, for storage of overwhelming feelings.

   • A filing cabinet located in a vault, for organizing information related to the trauma.

   • A protective bubble located somewhere in the sky, to hold unpleasant body sensations.

   • Your container should have some way to be securely closed, and a way to be reopened, over which only you have control.

   • Draw a picture of your container.

3. Consider the location that would best suit your container.

4. Draw or paint the surroundings.

5. Fill in any features necessary to make your container more effective.

6. Describe your container in writing. Be as specific as possible about its physical characteristics and location. Be sure to explain all of the container's features and why they are significant to you.

7. Write out each necessary step that you must take in order to place overwhelming material into your container. For instance, you could close your eyes and imagine such a ritual:

8. First, you create a symbolic object to represent a dangerous or threatening thought, memory, or feeling:

- Carefully wrap the symbolic object up, label it, and close the package.

- Now open the container and place the package inside.

- Securely close the container and fasten any locks securely. Perhaps labeling the container with instructions: "to be opened in the service of my healing" or something meaningful to you.

CLINICIAN'S CORNER:
CLINICAL APPLICATION OF PORGES' POLYVAGAL THEORY

ICE WATER DIVING AND UNFREEZING THE "FREEZE RESPONSE"

Two definitions followed by an application:

> When mammals dive, they must cope with the problem of being denied an external source of oxygen. To do so, they rely on anatomical features and physiological responses that increase oxygen storage while reducing the use of oxygen for nonessential activities during a dive. Blood vessels supplying nonessential organs are constricted, redirecting blood to the oxygen-requiring brain and heart. Because it is supplying fewer organs with blood, the heart can beat more slowly (a condition known as bradycardia) while maintaining adequate blood pressure to the brain, the most metabolically sensitive organ; a further benefit of bradycardia is that the heart requires less oxygen as well. Diving bradycardia is an easily measured component of a group of reflexes that also include holding the breath (apnea) and peripheral vasoconstriction. Together these reflexes constitute the "diving response." (Hiebert & Burch, 2003)

Polyvagal refers to the dual role of the vagus nerve. The parasympathetic nervous system has two branches: the *dorsal vagal* that drives immobility (more primitive in evolution) and the *ventral vagal* that involves higher order functioning and supports social engagement (more recent in evolution). The Polyvagal nervous system includes:

1. **The *dorsal vagal*, a.k.a. "the primitive parasympathetic,"** is the dorsal branch of the tenth cranial nerve, the vagus nerve, emanating from the dorsal nucleus brain stem (reptilian brain), which drives the PNS response. The unmyelinated dorsal vagal branch:

   a. Exerts influence on digestion: At low to moderate levels, modulating normal gastro-intestinal activity; at higher levels of intensity, stimulating vomiting and diarrhea

   b. Activates the immobility response, which may include feelings of overwhelming helplessness and generalized immobilization — including bradycardia and musculoskeletal paralysis.

   c. Descends to the heart and lungs, slowing heart rate and/or restricting breathing to conserve oxygen — a response humans share with reptiles resembling the "diving reflex" that most likely evolved in mammals to control states of immobility (paralysis in the freeze response).

According to the theory, the dorsal vagal-mediated immobility response is programmed to execute in conditions of external threat, i.e. physical restraint and inescapable threat, as well as in response to internal threats such as illness and hypoxia. Once the external or internal threats are removed or resolved and the fear has dissipated, then the dorsal vagal system is programmed to disengage, restoring the organism to homeostasis. However, if the fear state continues, the immobilization response, along with energy conservation continues as well, i.e., these normally time-limited responses may become chronic, fear-conditioned states of dysregulation that drive and maintain the intractable symptoms of PTSD.

The dorsal vagal response gets activated in response to events that challenge our safety and overwhelm our capacity to effectively cope. If, at that time, motor activity to self-protect was initiated yet thwarted, underlying activation of the SNS is likely, which may result in high oscillation between the SNS and PNS activation, resulting in a shutdown of the freeze response, and extreme difficulty connecting to higher cortical functions. In the dorsal vagal state we are much less socially oriented; incapable of accurately sending or receiving coherent social cues; display decreased emotional responsiveness; tend toward dissociation and fragmentation; exhibit flat affect or even a deathlike mask appearance.

2. **The *ventral vagal system*, a.k.a. "the smart vagus,"** connects to the tenth cranial nerve, the Vagus nerve, and along with cranial nerves V, VII, IX and XI, supports the muscles of the neck, throat, mouth, ears, nose, and the overall face. Originating from the ventral brain stem, it allows us to perceive social cueing from others as well as send our own social signals through facial and emotional expression. Supporting face-to face communication and contact for social engagement, the ventral vagal system in humans seems a more sophisticated means of interpersonally communicating or negotiating our way through threat, going beyond the former fight/flight and freeze responses. However, when this "smart system" fails us, we revert to the more primitive sympathetic fight/flight response. And, if that fails, we further regress and resort to our most primitive, *dorsal vagal response,* reflecting immobility, frozenness, and/or dissociation.

   Based on the above explanation of the physiological underpinnings of the freeze response (in particular, a release of the inhibition function of the primitive parasympathetic — driven by the dorsal vagal nerve, emanating from the brain stem — when the immobility response is engaged), it follows that immersing one's face in a bowl of ice water should elicit the aforementioned primitive "dive response" (Hiebert & Burch, 2003). Theoretically, it seems an effective means of regulating emotions (Porges, Doussard-Roosevelt, & Maita, 1994). Anecdotally, it has proven an effective clinical intervention for regulating emotion — specifically, in preventing or bringing a client back from a dissociative or ruminative episode (Linehan, 2009).

REFERENCES

Hiebert, S. & Burch, E.(2003). Simulated Human Diving And Heart Rate: Making The Most Of The Diving Response As A Laboratory Exercise. *Adv Physio Educ* 27:130–145.

Linehan, M. (2009). Psychotherapy Networker Conference. Washington, DC

Porges, S.W. (1997). *Emotion: An Evolutionary By-Product of the Neural Regulation of the Autonomic Nervous System.* Carter, C.S., Kirkpatrick, B., & Lederhendler I.I (Eds.) The Integrative Neurobiology of Affiliation. *Annal of the New York Academy of Sciences.* Volume 807.

Solomon, M. & Siegel, D.J. *Healing Trauma: Attachment, Mind, Body, and Brain* W. W. Norton & Company, 2003

CLIENT HANDOUT: BOBBING FOR REALITY

(BY THE WAY, YOU'LL BE BOBBING IN ICE WATER)

Dissociation is a word that is used to describe the disconnection or lack of connection between things that are usually associated with each other . . . in severe forms this disconnection tends to interrupt the typically integrated functions of consciousness, awareness, memory, and identity. For example, someone might think about an event that was extremely distressing, but have absolutely no feelings connected to it. Conversely, one may feel intermittently "taken over" by feelings of terror, rage and/or sadness that really don't seem to fit the occasion. Someone may find him/herself doing something that (s)he would not ordinarily do, but feel compelled to do it anyway.

If you have felt any of those aforementioned, or similar states of confusion, distraction and/or detachment, then you may wish to experiment with "Bobbing for Reality."

Based on the physiological underpinnings of the freeze response (which always includes a dissociative component), it follows that immersing one's face in a bowl of ice water would illicit the "dive response" — a primitive physiological response that appears to be an effective means of regulating emotions — specifically, in preventing or bringing someone back from a dissociative or ruminative episode.

INSTRUCTIONS:

1. Fill up a large bowl with ice water.

2. Dunk your face for several seconds.

3. Remove your face from the bowl.

4. Reorient yourself to the present (Who are you? Where are you? When are you?)

5. You have approximately ten minutes of clarity, during which time you must decide whether or not you wish to return to perseverating, fantasizing, and/or ruminating on traumatic/distressing material, or if there is another activity that might be more helpful in maintaining your sanity at this time.

CLINICIAN'S CORNER: MEDICATION

The discussion section on medications usually begins something like this: "The current trend in clinical psychiatry utilizes polypharmacy in conjunction with psychosocial treatments . . ." And then go on to present the most recent data, methods, results, and limitations from the latest pharmacotherapy studies. All of which is extremely helpful and necessary information that unfortunately, you won't read here.

What is provided is a simple reference table of the most commonly prescribed medications for adults with Complex Post-Traumatic Stress Disorder and the general consensus from experts in psychiatry and traumatology, followed by the often overlooked class of psychoactive drugs, the "no free lunch drugs" — those for which *Big Pharma* provides neither education nor samples: vitamins and supplements. (Sorry, no pens either.) Finally, recommended readings on traditional, complementary, and alternative medications in the treatment of traumatized clients.

Drug Class	Brand Name	Generic Name	Mechanism of Action
Antidepressants			
Multiple Reuptake Inhibitors Antidepressants	Cymbalta Desyrel Effexor Pristiq Remeron	Duloxetine Trazodone Venlafaxine Desvenlafaxine Mirtazapine	Affects the concentration of the neurotransmitters serotonin and/or norepinephrine, chemicals in the brain thought to be linked to anxiety .
Selective Serotonin Reuptake Inhibitors (SSRIs)	Celexa Lexapro Luvox Paxil Prozac Zoloft	Citalopram Escitalopram Fluvoxamine Paroxetine Fluoxetine Sertraline	Affects the concentration and activity of the neurotransmitter sero-tonin, a chemical in the brain thought to be linked to anxiety disorders.
Monoamine Oxidase Inhibitors (MAOIs)	Marplan Nardil Parnate	Isocarboxazide Phenelzine Tranylcypromine	Blocks the effect of an important brain enzyme, preventing the breakdown of serotonin and norepinephrine.

Drug Class	Brand Name	Generic Name	Mechanism of Action
Anxiolytics			
Azapirones	BuSpar	Buspirone	Enhances the activity of serotonin.
Anticonvulsants			
	Gabitril Neurontin	Tiagabine Gabapentin	Enhances the function of GABA. These medications may be added when symptoms only partially respond to another medication to increase the overall response to treatment.
	Depakote Lamictal Topamax	Valproate Lamotrigine Topiramate	Exact mechanisms unknown. Possible effects include: enhancing or inhibiting effects of neuro-transmitters believed to be associated with anxiety; blocking of sodium channels in the brain.
Noradrenergic Agents			
Beta Blockers	Inderal Tenormin	Propranolol Atenolol	Blocks receptors associated with physiologic symptoms of anxiety.
Alpha Blocker	Minipress Catapres Tenex	Clonidine Prazosin Guanfacine	Blocks receptors associated with physiologic symptoms of anxiety.
Atypical Antipsychotics			
	Abilify Geodon Risperdal Seroquel Zyprexa	Aripiprazole Ziprasidone Risperidone Quetiapine Olanzapine	These medications may be added when symptoms only partially respond to another medication to increase the overall response to treatment. Affects the concentration and activity of the neurotransmitter serotonin, a chemical in the brain thought to be linked to anxiety disorders.

Medication Recommendations

1. Any/all psychoactive medication should be used in conjunction with psychotherapy, never as a replacement.

2. Although compliance is often an issue, inform the client that the recommendations for antidepressant use is a therapeutic trial of 12 weeks before changing the regimen. (Realize that this may be a tough sell, as sometimes clients experience side effects worse than the symptoms being treated), therefore it is important to discuss medication options and compliance issues at each visit.

   - Strongly recommend norepinephrine and serotonin reuptake inhibitors.

   - Strongly recommend selective serotonin reuptake inhibitors (SSRIs) for the treatment of PTSD.

   - Recommend tricyclic antidepressants (TCAs) and monoamine oxidase inhibitors (MAOIs) as second-line treatments for PTSD.

   - Consider a second-generation (e.g., nefazodone, trazodone, venlafaxine, mirtazapine, bupropion, etc) in the management of PTSD. Trazadone is especially attractive given its additional sedative properties.

   - Consider prazosin to augment the management of nightmares and other re-experiencing symptoms.

   - There is growing evidence to support use of mood stabilizers (e.g., lamotrigine) for the treatment of PTSD.

   - There is growing evidence to support use of atypical antipsychotics.

   - Recommend against the long-term use of benzodiazepines to manage core symptoms in PTSD.

   - Recommend against typical antipsychotics in the management of PTSD.

Psychiatric Medications Through The Trauma Lens

Featuring Frank Guastella Anderson, M.D.

This video presentation of one of our most popular workshops discusses medications for PTSD, dissociation, and associated symptoms, for both children and adults. Non-prescribing clinicians will gain greater understanding of the role of medication in addressing the biological substrates of trauma response, and different goals of various medication categories; psychopharmacologists will learn about the latest research from an expert in the field. This presentation also includes an overview of alternatives to traditional treatments as well as medications that are being newly developed for trauma. This 2-DVD series, with total running time of 2 hours, 33 minutes.

To Obtain Assessment Materials:

Website: www.traumacenter.org/products/psychmed_video.php

BUT WHAT IF MY CLIENT WON'T TAKE THEM?

Some clients won't. Some adamantly refuse to be prescribed psychiatric medications. To be candid, if/when clients are thorough enough in their investigation of the medications, they can usually present a fairly cogent argument against their use. *(For further information the reader is referred to: Jackson, G., Rethinking Psychiatric Drugs: A Guide for Informed Consent Authorhouse, (2005))*

Some consider medications a crutch; something they would not need if they were not "so weak". Clients with histories of substance abuse (particularly those involved in 12-step groups) may consider psychiatric medication a compromise to their sobriety. Some have previously taken meds that resulted in a deterioration rather than improvement of their symptomology. Some have been told horror stories. Others can't bear the sexual side effects. Some belong to religious groups and/or families who may disapprove. (One client reported that he had read over ninety untoward side effects of a certain medication for depression. He decided to keep reading as the words scrolled down the TV screen because the advertisement was for the drug that both his psychiatrist and I had recommended. [Just a reminder that sometimes safety issues look like paranoia, and sometimes clinicians look like perpetrators.])

It's obvious that there are reasons to anticipate that not every client will be "open" the suggestion. Regardless of the origin of the resistance, it is crucial that clinicians recognize and empathically validate clients' core concern(s). Within the course of therapy, psychoeducation regarding pharmacotherapy and its benefits (and costs) may be helpful, but it is important that the client not feel disempowered. It is essential that clinicians realize that power struggles are categorically lose/lose situations. The decision to take medication is the client's and any degree of coercion is likely to be experienced as a traumatic relational reenactment.

If the resistance is about medication, per se, clinicians can offer alternatives. If we look at the types of medications recommended above and understand how they affect brain chemistry to treat the symptom clusters associated with PTSD, it's not unfathomable that other chemicals (perhaps through the same mechanism, perhaps not) may produce similar results. (For the record, this author has always subscribed to the "better life through chemistry" dictum, but *Big Pharma* doesn't own chemistry.) Below is a list of vitamins and supplements that alternative/complementary physicians commonly recommend. The idea is to treat the arousal symptoms initially, and then move to address the depressive symptoms.

Relaxation Supplements		
Supplement	Dosage	Frequency
Tryptophan	500–5000 mg	Daily
5HTP	50–800 mg 50–100 mg (if using with SSRI)	Daily
Melatonin	4–8 mg	At bedtime
Methionine	Up to 200 mg	At bedtime
NAC (n-acetyl-cysteine)	1–5 gm	Daily
Taurine (MagTaurate)	500 mg	2–6x daily
Glutamine	1–2 heaping tsp(s)	Daily
Theanine	Up to 300 mg	2x daily
GABA	Up to 1500 mg	2x daily
Glycine (MagGlycinate)	Up to 1 tsp	2x daily
Lecithin	1 gm	2–5x daily
Optizync (Zinc Methionate)	1 capsule	2x daily
Iron Glycinate	< 50 mg	Daily
Potassium	Follow manufacturer's recommendations	
Energizing Supplement		
Supplement	Dosage	Frequency
Tyrosine	500–3000 mg	2x daily
DLPA	500–2000 mg	2x daily
Selenium (Selenomethionine)	200 mg	2x daily
SAMe	400 mg	2–5x daily
DMAE	Up to 500 mg	Daily
Iodine/Kelp	2 capsules	With meals
B Complex & P5P	50 mg	2x daily
Multimineral supplement	2 capsules	With meals
Vitamin C (buffered as Calcium Magnesium, Potasium ascorbate)	1000–4000 mg	2x daily as tolerated

For further information the reader is referred to:

COMPLEMENTARY AND ALTERNATIVE MEDICINE AND PSYCHIATRY

The book is written from the perspective of clinicians who practice in both traditional and alternative medicine. The book covers the major areas in CAM, including herbal medicine and nutrients, acupuncture, meditative therapies, and yoga. It provides the most important and up-to-date scientific data, along with controversies that exist in the field.

TO OBTAIN MATERIALS:

Complementary and Alternative Medicine and Psychiatry by Philip R. Muskin, published by American Psychiatric Pub, 2000

NATURAL MEDICATIONS FOR PSYCHIATRIC DISORDERS

Updated for its second edition, this book is the only reference to focus exclusively on natural medications in psychiatry. Eminent psychiatrists from the Massachusetts General Hospital and other leading institutions examine current scientific and clinical data on the applications, effectiveness, and safety of natural psychotropics and acupuncture. Quick-reference tabular appendices list indications, contraindications, dosages, combinations, and drug-drug interactions for each remedy. This edition includes brand-new chapters on acupuncture, homeopathy, and therapies for substance dependence and weight management. The chapter on polypharmacy and side effect management addresses the growing issue of drug-drug interactions. New introductory chapters discuss complementary and alternative medicine in society and examine research limitations and quality assurance issues.

TO OBTAIN MATERIALS:

Natural Medications for Psychiatric Disorders: Considering the Alternatives by David Mischoulon, Jerrold F. Rosenbaum, published by Lippincott, Williams, and Wilkins, 2008

STAGE TWO: WORKING THROUGH TRAUMA

CLINICIAN'S CORNER:
MAKING TRAUMA THERAPY SAFE:
THE BODY AS RESOURCE FOR BRAKING TRAUMATIC ACCELERATION

©1997 Babette Rothschild, MSW, LCSW from Self and Society May 1999

Traumatic events exact a toll on the body as well as the mind. This is a well documented and agreed upon conclusion of the psychiatric community as attested in the diagnostic and statistical manual of the American Psychiatric Association. A major category in their symptom list of post-traumatic stress disorder (PTSD) is "persistent symptoms of increased arousal" in the autonomic nervous system (ANS) (APA 1994). Yet, despite a plethora of study and writing since PTSD first appeared as a diagnostic category 17 years ago (APA 1980), there has been little attention given to this, the somatic side of trauma. The attention that has been given to the body tends to focus on the distressing symptoms of PTSD and the resulting problems. Consideration of using the body, itself, as a possible resource in the treatment of trauma has rarely been explored. The consequences of such an exclusion are multifold as comprehending traumatic impact on the body may be a vital key to understanding and treating the traumatized body as well as the traumatized mind. Moreover, somatic interventions may be useful as an adjunct to existing trauma therapies, making the therapy easier to pace, and less volatile. This article will review the phenomenon of "increased arousal" in the ANS and present several somatic techniques that are useful in stopping or reducing ANS hyperarousal.

INTRODUCTION

Most of my psychotherapy colleagues and professional workshop participants tell me that they know all too well just how tricky psychotherapy with trauma can be — regardless of the theory or techniques that are being applied. The risk of client overwhelm, anxiety and panic attacks, flashbacks, or worse re-traumatization, always lingers. I have heard reports of clients getting such overwhelming flashbacks during therapy sessions, that the treatment room became misinterpreted as the site of the trauma and the therapist the perpetrator of the trauma. Reports of clients becoming unable to function normally in their daily lives during a course of trauma therapy — some even requiring hospitalization — are not uncommon. Working with trauma seems, universally, to be rather more precarious than other realms of psychotherapy.

I have found it safest to approach trauma therapy in a similar way that I approach driving an automobile. My logic stems from the observation that both driving and trauma therapy involve controlling something that can easily go out of control.

I've taught several friends to drive. I always begin the same way. First, before my driving student is allowed to cause the car to move forward, I teach him how to stop, how to brake. It is only once my student (and I) are secure in his ability to find the brake pedal and stop the car reflexively, that I deem it safe for him to meet the accelerator and learn to (slowly) advance the car, while periodically returning to the brake pedal — stop and go. Safe driving involves timely and careful braking combined with acceleration at the rate that the traffic, driver and vehicle can bear. So does safe trauma therapy.

It is not a good idea to proceed with directly addressing a traumatic incident — accelerating trauma processes in the mind and body — unless both you and your client know how to apply the brakes: stop that process if it becomes too uncomfortable or destabilizing. Safe trauma therapy includes: 1) understanding the phenomenon of hyperarousal, 2) the ability to observe and gauge the state of the ANS, and 3) body oriented tools for stopping, containing and reducing hyperarousal — applying the brakes.

ANS and the Physiology of Hyperarousal

Notice what you feel in your body, particularly your heart rate and breathing as you read the following:

> Imagine you wake in the middle of the night to the sound of shattering glass. You think of the front door with the glass pane in the middle. You are immediately alert. You hold your breath. Your heart pounds. You go carefully into the hall, all senses heightened, eyes wide. Proceeding towards the front door, you find a vase in pieces on the floor, your cat skulking guiltily away. You exhale, and then yell at the cat, your heart rate comes back to normal, and you shake just a little bit for a few minutes.

> The limbic system of the brain responds to extreme stress/trauma/threat by releasing hormones that tell the body to prepare for defensive action, activating the sympathetic branch (SNS) of the autonomic nervous system (ANS), preparing the body for fight or flight: increasing respiration and heart rate, sending blood away from the skin and into the muscles, etc. When threat is imminent or prolonged (as with torture, rape, etc.), the brain can also release hormones to heighten the parasympathetic branch (PNS) of the ANS, and tonic immobility — like a mouse going dead (slack) or a frog or bird becoming paralyzed (stiff) — can result. (Gallup 1977, Levine 1997)

With PTSD the brain continues to respond as if under stress/trauma/threat, continuing to prepare the body for fight/flight, or going dead (sometimes called "freezing") even though the actual traumatic event has ended. People with PTSD live with a chronic state of ANS activation — hyperarousal — in their bodies leading to physical symptoms that include: anxiety, panic, muscle stiffness, weakness, exhaustion, concentration problems, sleep disturbance, etc.

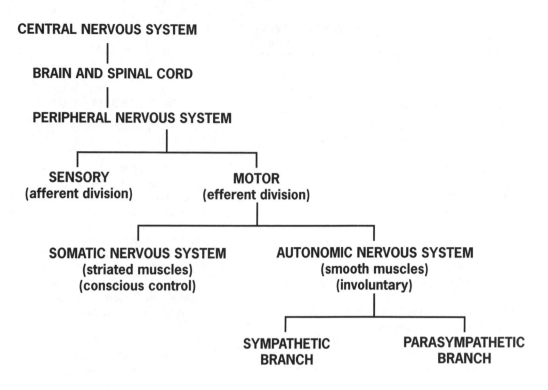

Diagram 1. Illustrates the organization of the body's nervous system

During a traumatic event the brain tells the body there is threat. In PTSD, the body persists in telling the brain there is continued threat; the brain continues to stimulate the ANS for defense. It is a vicious circle. Objects, sounds, colors, movements, etc., that might otherwise be insignificant, become associated to the trauma and become external triggers that are experienced internally as danger (van der Kolk 1996). Confusion can result when recognition of external safety does not coincide with the inner experience of threat. Hyperarousal can become chronic, or can be triggered acutely. Breaking this cycle is an important step in the treatment of PTSD.

The ability to recognize indications of hyperarousal, that is, ANS over-activation can help in breaking that cycle. It is easy to learn, but as with any skill it takes a degree of practice. I suggest that all professionals (psychotherapists, and body workers alike) working with traumatized clients — no matter what theory base or techniques are being used — memorize the signs for both SNS, PNS and combined activation and practice observing them in others. It is also very useful to ask your client periodically what he is aware of in his heart rate, breathing, etc. — particularly those ANS signs that are more difficult to observe. By noticing what is happening in the client, the psychotherapist secures a valuable, objective gauge for reading the arousal state of the client. It can also be useful to teach the client to recognize signs of ANS activation in himself — he will gain a greater sense of body awareness and a greater sense of self-knowledge and self-control.

AUTONOMIC NERVOUS SYSTEM
(smooth muscles)
(involuntary)

SYMPATHETIC BRANCH	PARASYMPATHETIC BRANCH
Activates during stress states, including, but not only, traumatic events	Activates during states of rest and relaxation
Noticeable signs: Faster respiration Quicker heart rate (pulse) Increased blood pressure Pupils dilate Pale skin color Increased sweating Skin cold (possibly clammy) to touch Digestion (and peristalsis) decreases	**Noticeable signs:** Slower, deeper respiration Slower heart rate (pulse) Decreased blood pressure Pupils constrict Blushed/flushed skin color Skin warm (usually dry) to touch Digestion (and peristalsis) increases
During actual traumatic event OR with flashback (visual, auditory, and/or sensory): Preparation for quick movement leading to possible fight reflex or flight reflex	**During actual traumatic event OR with flashback (visual, auditory and/or sensory):** Can also activate concurrently, while masking sympathetic activation, leading to tonic immobility; freezing reflex (like a mouse, caught by a cat, going dead), marked by simultaneous signs of high sympathetic and parasympathetic activation.

Diagram 2. Illustrates the organization of the autonomic nervous system

The PNS and SNS branches of the ANS function in balance with each other. The SNS is primarily aroused in states of stress, both positive and negative. Examples of positive experiences that create stress in the body include: orgasm, getting married, or a challenging sport. Stress can also be the result of pressured expectations at work or school, financial problems, family conflicts, etc. The most extreme stress is traumatic stress as the result of threat to life. The PNS is primarily aroused in states of rest and relaxation, pleasure, sexual arousal, etc. Both branches are always engaged, but one is usually more active, the other suppressed — like a scale: when one side is up, the other is down. They constantly swing in complementary balance to each other (Bloch 1985). The following will illustrate the interactive balance of the SNS and PNS:

> You are sleeping restfully, the PNS is active and the SNS suppressed, you awaken and find you set the clock wrong and you are already one hour late for work. The SNS shoots up: your heart rate accelerates, you are instantly awake. You move quickly showering, dressing then running for the bus. When you get to the bus stop you notice the clock on the church tower and realize this was the weekend that winter time started, and actually you aren't late after all. The SNS decreases and the PNS rises. Your heart rate slows, you breathe easier. But when you get to work, you find you forgot a deadline and scurry to catch up before your boss finds out. The SNS again accelerates, suppressing the PNS. You work quickly . . .

So it goes throughout the average day with the SNS and PNS swaying in balance with each other.

Applying ANS Knowledge in the Therapy Setting

A major advantage of learning to observe the bodily signs of ANS activation is having additional tools to help clients contain and reduce hyperarousal in their daily lives, as well as avoiding this highly traumatized (and possibly retraumatizing) state during therapy sessions.

PNS activation (slow respiration, slow heart rate, contracted pupils, etc.) indicates the client is relaxed, and the therapy is progressing at a comfortable rate. Low SNS activation (increased respiration, increased heart rate, dilated pupils, etc.) Indicates excitement and/or containable discomfort. High SNS activation (rapid heart rate, hyperventilation, etc.) may mean the client is having trouble dealing with what is going on and may be quite anxious. And when high sympathetic activation becomes masked by high parasympathetic activation (and there are indications that both are aroused simultaneously — i.e., pale skin with slow breathing, dilated eyes with flushed skin, slow heart rate and rapid breathing, etc.), the client is in a highly traumatized state and it is time to hit the brakes. He is likely experiencing some type of flashback (in images, body sensations, emotions, or a combination). In such an instance, the therapist must help stabilize the client — as indicated by either lowered sympathetic activation or primarily parasympathetic activation — before proceeding further with the therapeutic work or sending him home. Not to do so could risk panic, re-traumatization, breakdown, or worse. Several strategies useful for accomplishing such stabilization are addressed in the next section.

Caution: not all of the following techniques will work for all clients. Some clients may find one or more of them provoking rather than containing. Experiment slowly using bodyawareness and drop any technique that increases anxiety or symptoms.

Somatic Resources For Braking: Slowing Down And Containing Hyperarousal

Bodyawareness

Being able to accurately sense what is happening in one's body appears to be a powerful tool in trauma therapy for braking though it can also be accessed to enable acceleration of the therapy process (when the client is ready) as a catalyst to somatic memory (van der Kolk 1994). Client skill in bodyawareness will make the other techniques described below more effective. "bodyawareness" in this usage — as taught in the bodynamic training programs (bodynamic institute 1988-1992) — refers to the precise awareness of the physical body: skin, muscles, bones, organs, breathing, movement, position in space, etc. It further implies how the body is actually being experienced/sensed in the here-and-now: temperature, tension/relaxation, pain, prickles, pressure, size, humidity (i.e., sweating hands), heart rate, "growling stomach", vibration, etc. Contrary to what you might think, clients usually become less, rather than more anxious when encouraged to notice and describe their bodily sensations (but there are exceptions to this rule — bodyawareness is not for everybody). Once they get the hang of it, many clients report that during trauma therapy, it is a relief for them to be periodically asked about their bodyawareness — the bodyawareness can become a secure resource in itself.

Not every client can use this braking tool, though. There are several situations where it would be contraindicated. Two examples: 1) some traumas are so damaging to the bodily integrity that any sensing of the body over-accelerates contact to the trauma(s); 2) there are also clients who will feel pressured to sense their body "correctly" — a kind of performance anxiety can develop. In such cases it is better to bypass training in bodyawareness and use other braking techniques instead.

Tensing Peripheral Muscles — Holding Together

Tensing in peripheral muscles of arms and legs is often calming and containing. Tensing is a particularly useful braking technique and is usually very effective for reducing hyperarousal, or at least making it seem more containable. The principles for this were taught to me in the bodynamic training program (1988-1992), as well as the leg exercises. The arm exercises were taught to me by my colleague, physical therapist and body-psychotherapist, Robyn Bohen (Bohen 1991).

Important: any tensing should be done only until the muscle feels slightly tired. Release of the tensing must be done very, very slowly. Try one tensing and evaluate with bodyawareness before going on to the next. If tensing causes any adverse reaction (nausea, spaciness, anxiety, etc.), you can usually neutralize the reaction by gently stretching the same muscle — making an opposite movement.

- Legs: stand with feet a little less than shoulder-width apart, knees relaxed (neither locked, nor bent). Press knees out directly to the side so that you can feel tension along the sides of the legs from knee to hip.
- Left arm: sit or stand with arms crossed right over left. The right hand should be covering the left elbow.
- The right hand provides resistance as the left arm lifts directly away from the body. You should feel tension in the forward directed part of the upper arm from shoulder to elbow.
- The right hands provide resistance to the back of the elbow as the left arm pushes directly left. You should feel tension in the left-directed part of the upper arm from shoulder to elbow.
- Right arm: sit or stand with arms crossed left over right. The left hand should be covering the right elbow.
- The left hand provides resistance as the right arm lifts directly away from the body. You should feel tension in the forward directed part of the upper arm from shoulder to elbow.
- The left hands provide resistance to the back of the elbow as the right arm pushes directly right. You should feel tension in the right-directed part of the upper arm from shoulder to elbow.

Dual Awareness

A few years ago, in a professional workshop I was asked the following question by a psychotherapist participant: "what do I do about a client who, as soon as she enters the therapy room goes into flashback, believing the therapy room to be the scene of the trauma and me to be the perpetrator?" my answer was simple, "stop her!" Of course, sometimes this is easier said then done.

In my experience it is not possible for a client to work through a trauma until and unless he can maintain a dual awareness of past and present. I have found that allowing a client to continue in flashback and hyperarousal only adds to his experience of trauma and sense of hopelessness to overcome it.

Sometimes you have to work with a client for a period of time (weeks, months, and years) before he has enough ego strength to be able to maintain this dual awareness while addressing the trauma. When this is the case, that must be the prerequisite focus of the therapy. Once the client has developed this capacity, the use of dual awareness, it can also be used as a braking tool. This is a great asset. Bessel van der Kolk discusses the difference between the "experiencing self" and the "observing self" in the traumatized client (van der Kolk 1996b). In a traumatized person, there may be a marked split. Teaching the client to acknowledge both parts by stating the reality of both selves at the same time, is often a key to calm.

Acknowledging this split has helped several of my Danish clients to wait for the train in the one underground station in Copenhagen, Airport, where they otherwise were prone to anxiety attacks. This simple technique involves accepting and stating (aloud or in thought) the reality of both the experiencing self and the observing self at the same time: "I'm feeling very scared here (experiencing self)," while at the same time actually looking around, evaluating the situation, and if it is true, saying,"but I'm not in any danger (observing self)."

It's also an effective technique for stopping a flashback: "I am feeling very [insert emotion, usually scared] right now because i am remembering [insert traumatic event] . . . and I am looking around and can see that [insert traumatic event] is not happening right now."

Establishing a Sense of Boundary at the Skin Level

Much trauma is the result of events that were in one way or another physically invasive: assault, rape, car accidents, surgery, torture, beatings, etc. Often it is loss of the sense of bodily integrity that accelerates a trauma process out of control. Reestablishing the sense of boundary at the skin level will often reduce hyperarousal. To increase the sense of bodily integrity, I will often suggest that a client physically feel his/her periphery/boundary — the skin. This can be done in two ways:

1. Have your client use his own hand to rub firmly (not too light, not too hard) over his surface. Try one spot, e.g. An arm or leg, first. If it is containing and calming for the client, go on to another place, eventually covering the entire body. Make sure the rubbing stays on the surface — skin (clothes over skin), and does not become a gripping or massaging of muscles. If your client doesn't like touching himself, he can use a wall or door (often a cold wall is great) to rub against or have him use a pillow or towel to make the contact. Remember, especially, the back, and the sides of the arms and legs.

2. Some clients will feel too provoked even touching their own skin. In that case it might work to have them sense their skin through sensing the objects they are in contact with. Have the person feel where his buttocks meet the chair; his feet meet the inside of his shoes, the palms of his/her hands rest on his thighs, etc. As the client tries either of these, it may be useful to have him thinking or saying to himself "this is me", "this is where I stop", etc.

Feeling the boundary of the skin can serve as a braking technique for many. But note, for some this technique will be more provoking than calming; use caution.

Feeling the Solidness of the Bones

Some people who become provoked when feeling their skin may respond well to feeling the solidness of their bones (caution, though, as a few could be frightened by this — bones remind some of skeletons and death). Sensing the spine, in particular, can be a great aid to braking. This can be done sitting or standing, placing the spine against a wall or out-facing corner. It can also be done without outside contact by focusing on the internal support of the spine. Ask your client if he can feel his spine supporting his trunk to stay upright.

You can also offer your client a wooden spoon or pencil to tap gently on bone projections at elbow and wrist, or knee and ankle — it helps to know a little anatomy if you use this one so you can guide your client to tapping the proximal and distal ends of the same bone. When done correctly, the client will feel a vibration along the length of the bone. For many, this has a very solidifying — and braking — effect, reducing or stopping hyperarousal.

Conclusion

Observation of the ANS combined with simple somatic techniques can be an effective adjunct in the containment and reduction of traumatic symptoms, making trauma therapy safer and less traumatic.

REFERENCES

American Psychiatric Association (APA), *Diagnostic And Statistical Manual Of Mental Disorders,* Third Edition, 1980.

American Psychiatric Association (APA), *Diagnostic And Statistical Manual Of Mental Disorders,* Forth Edition, 1994.

Bloch, George, Ph.D., *Body And Self: Elements Of Human Biology, Behavior And Health.* William Kaufmann, Inc 1985

Brett, EA, "The Classification Of Post-traumatic Stress Disorder," In van der Kolk, BA, Mcfarlane, AC, & Weisaeth, L (Eds.) *Traumatic Stress,* Guilford Press 1996.

Diamond, MC, Scheibel, AB, & Elson, LM, *The Human Brain Coloring Book,* Harper Perennial 1985.

Gallup, Gordon G., Jr., And Maser, Jack D., "Tonic Immobility: Evolutionary Underpinnings Of Human Catalepsy And Catatonia", In Seligman, Martin E. P., And Masser, Jack D., *Psychopathology: Experimental Models*, San Francisco: W.H. Freeman And Company, 1977.

Levine, Peter, Ph.D., *Waking The Tiger*, 1997

Ornstein, Robert & Thompson, Richard, *The Amazing Brain*, Houghton Mifflin, Usa, 1986

Rothschild, Babette, M.S.W., "A Shock Primer For The Bodypsychotherapist," *Energy And Character,* Vol. 24, No. 1, April 1993.

Rothschild, Babette, M.S.W., "Defining Shock And Trauma In Bodypsychotherapy," *Energy And Character,* Vol. 26, No.2, September 1995.

Rothschild, Babette, M.S.W., "Applying The Brakes: Theory And Tools For Understanding, Slowing Down And Reducing Autonomic Nervous System Activation In Traumatized Clients," Paper Presented At The Tenth Scandinavian Conference For Psychotherapists Working With Traumatized Refugees, 24–26 May 1996, Åbo, Finland.

Rothschild, Babette, M.S.W., "A Trauma Case History," *Somatics,* Fall 1996/Spring 1997.

Rothschild, Babette, M.S.W., "Slowing Down And Controlling Traumatic Hyperarousal," In, Vanderberger, L (Ed.) *The Many Faces Of Trauma, International Perspectives* (In Press). 1997

van der Kolk, Bessel, M.D. (1996a), "The Body Keeps The Score," *Harvard Psychiatric Review*, Vol. 1, 1994.

van der Kolk, BA, Mcfarlane, AC, & Weisaeth, L (Eds.) *Traumatic Stress,* Guilford Press

Babette Rothschild, MSW, LCSW, has been a clinical social worker since 1976 and a teacher and trainer since 1992. She is the author of three books, all published by WW Norton: *The Body Remembers — The Psychophysiology of Trauma and Trauma Treatment* (a bestseller); *The Body Remembers Casebook — Unifying Methods and Models in the Treatment of Trauma and PTSD*; *Help for the Helper — The Psychophysiology of Compassion Fatigue and Vicarious Trauma*; and *8 Keys to Safe Trauma Recovery*.

This article has been reproduced with Ms. Rothschild's generous permission. Her websites are: http://www.trauma.cc, and www.safetraumarecovery.com. She may be contacted at: 310.281.9646, or babette@trauma.cc.

Working Through Trauma: Mindfulness

Between stimulus and response there is a space. In that space is our power to choose our response. In our response lies our growth and our freedom.

— Viktor E. Frankl

The Theory

In his work, *The Mindful Brain*, Daniel Siegel explains how consciousness plays a direct role in the harnessing of neural plasticity (the brain's ability to alter automatic modes of neural firing which enables new patterns of neural firing to occur). He writes, "The basic steps linking consciousness with neural plasticity are as follows: Where attention goes, neural firing occurs. And where neurons fire, new connections can be made. In this manner, learning a new way to pay attention within the integration of consciousness enables an open receptive mind within therapy to catalyze the integration of new combinations of previously isolated segments of our mental reality." One way to practice this "new way of paying attention within the integration of consciousness" is through a mindful practice.

While other clinicians are discovering the benefits and have begun to incorporate mindfulness into their own clinical work, some pioneer clinicians have been doing it for years — most notably, Kabat-Zinn's work, *Mindfulness-Based Stress Reduction*; Brach's *Radical Acceptance* and Linehan's *Dialectical Behavior Therapy*. For further information on these pioneers and their work the reader should visit the websites and refer to the literature below:

- Tara Brach: http://www.imcw.org/getcat.php?cid=11

  Radical Acceptance: Embracing Your Life with the Heart of a Buddha
  Radical Acceptance: Awakening the Love That Heals Fear and Shame

- Marsha Linehan: http://faculty.washington.edu/linehan/

  Skills Training Manual for Treating Borderline Personality Disorder

- Jon Kabat-Zinn: http://www.umassmed.edu/behavmed/faculty/kabat-zinn.cfm

  Wherever You Go, There You Are: Mindfulness Meditation in Everyday Life
  Coming to Our Senses: Healing Ourselves and the World Through Mindfulness

During trauma, dissociation provides a psychological escape when physical escape is not an option. Quite a gift, really. Another gift for the survivor would be a practice that provided a means for the development of a healthier escape-a conscious detachment and *dis-identification* from trauma's sequelae. Mindfulness and mindfulness meditation is such a practice.

In meditation, the survivor detaches and observes his/her internal process, as (s)he is experiencing it. Detachment from feelings, sensations and thoughts, allows emotional and physical pain to become more distant, therefore more manageable. Only when the survivor no longer identifies with the suffering, can (s)he transcend or transform it.

Mindfulness is a technique that cultivates an intentional awareness of the present moment. It helps clients experience life non-judgmentally, as it unfolds moment by moment, with curiosity, attention, and compassion for self and others. Engaging in life mindfully helps clients to develop more skillful and creative responses to life — to live with greater balance and ease; to cope with life's stressors and challenges; to accept the human condition; and to develop an awareness of, and appreciation for, the only time we have: the now. As previously stated, mindfulness is attracting increasing interest among western psychiatrists as a non-pharmacological means of dealing with anxiety and depressive mood states.

Meditation affects the body in exactly the opposite ways that traumatic symptoms do. When practicing meditation, heart rate and breathing slow down; blood pressure normalizes; oxygen is used more efficiently; adrenal glands produce less cortisol, adrenaline and noradrenalin; positive hormone production increases; and immune function improves. In addition, the mind gains clarity and creativity increases. People who meditate find it easier to give up former coping mechanisms, i.e., life-damaging habits like smoking, drinking, bingeing, purging, self-injury and drugs. Meditation restores the body to a calm state, helps the body to physically repair itself, and prevents new damage caused by the physical effects of every day stress.

According to Thich Nhat Hanh — Buddhist monk, poet, scholar, peace activist and one of the best-known teachers of mindfulness today — "Awareness of breathing and of our steps is our anchor in the present moment. It enables us to nourish peace, joy, love and understanding in our individual and collective consciousness, and to avoid losing ourselves in regrets about the past, worries about the future, or craving, anger, or jealousy in the present." Hanh offers a practice of mindfulness that seems to appeal to Western sensibilities. His contribution permeates the work of Jon Kabat-Zinn, Tara Brach, Jack Kornfield and Marsha Linehan

Sharon Salzberg, cofounder of the Insight Meditation Society, writes, "The entire purpose of meditation practice is to learn how to harness, refine, and sensitize this quite incredible power of awareness." According to Hahn, "The miracle is not to walk on water. The miracle is to walk on the green earth in the present moment, to appreciate the peace and beauty that are available now. Hanh's teachings are very simple and easy to instruct others in the practice. Below are examples of his mindfulness breathing techniques from Touching Peace, Parallax Press, 1992, p. 1.

Thich Nhat Hanh: Buddhist monk, poet, scholar, peace activist, and one of the best known teachers of mindfulness today. (http://www.plumvillage.org/)

Books:
- *Buddha Mind, Buddha Body: Walking Towards Enlightenment*
- *No Death, No Fear: Comforting Wisdom for Life*
- *Touching Peace*

(Thich Nhat Hanh has written over seventy books. For a complete list, please visit http://www.parallax.org/index.html)

SIMPLE BREATH MEDITATIONS

As you inhale, say to yourself,

> *"Breathing in, I know that I am breathing in," or simply "In."*

As you exhale, say to yourself,

> *"Breathing out, I know that I am breathing out," or simply "Out."*

With this exercise you recognize your in-breath as an in-breath and your out-breath as an out-breath. This technique can help keep the mind on the breath. The mind becomes peaceful and gentle along with the breath. It takes but a few minutes to experience the benefits of this meditation. It is important and enjoyable to breathe in and out. The breath links the body to the mind.

Recite this line and feel the coolness permeate your body, just like a cool drink on a hot day. When you breathe in and recite this line, you can feel the breath calming the body and mind.

When the mind is thinking one thing and the body is doing another, mind and body are disconnected.

By concentrating on breathing "In" and "Out," we reconnect mind and body and become integrated and whole again.

> *"Breathing in, I calm my body."*
>
> *"Breathing out, I smile."*

A smile can relax hundreds of facial muscles.

Smiling shows that you are master of yourself.

> *"Dwelling in the present moment."*

With this phrase you can sit. You don't need to think of anything else.

You know exactly where you are.

> *"I know this is a wonderful moment."*

It is wonderful to sit, stable and at ease. It is a joy to return to your breath, to smile, and to know your true nature.

Our appointment with life is in the present moment.

If you do not have peace and joy right now, when will you have it? What prevents you from being happy right now? Follow your breath and say, simply,

> *"Calming. Smiling. Present moment. Wonderful moment."*

CLIENT HANDOUT: BREATHING PACKET

The "I think" which Kant said must be able to accompany all my objects, is the "I breathe" which actually does accompany them.

— William James

Breathing is so simple and so obvious we often take it for granted; ignoring the power it has to affect body, mind, and spirit. As you begin to become mindful of your breathing, you may notice that even at rest your breathing is faster than the "average" rate of 12 to 14 times a minute. Hans Weller queried, "Nearly every physical problem is accompanied by a disturbance of breathing. But which comes first?" Well, the fact is that many of us habitually 'hyperventilate'; we typically breathe rapidly and shallowly — from the top of our chest only. This kind of breathing sharply reduces the level of carbon dioxide in our blood, causing arteries — including the carotid artery going to the brain — to constrict, thus reducing the flow of blood to the rest of the body. So, unfortunately it doesn't really matter how much oxygen we breathe into our lungs, because our brain and body inevitably perceive a shortage of oxygen. In turn, this shortage of oxygen activates our sympathetic nervous system's fight or flight response" — producing tension, anxiety, irritability, and a marked impairment in our ability to process information.

The key to slowing down our breathing is not to try to purposely slow it down, but rather to learn to breathe more deeply, using our diaphragm, belly, rib cage, and lower back in the breathing process. To do belly/abdominal/diaphragmatic breathing properly allow your lungs to fill from the bottom up. On inhalation, the diaphragm and the muscles between your ribs contract and expand the chest cavity, lowering the pressure in the chest cavity. Room air then flows in through the airways (from high pressure to low pressure) and inflates the lungs. On exhalation, the diaphragm and intercostal muscles relax and the size of the thorax decreases. The decrease in volume in the chest increases the pressure in the thorax above the outside air pressure. Air from the lungs (high pressure) then flows out of the airways to the outside air (low pressure). The cycle then repeats with each breath.

When breathing with only the top half of the chest, the top of the lungs open first, and air fills only those top segments. However, if you push your belly out during inhalation, then the diaphragm expands first. The lower ribs then push out and open the lower portions of the lungs first. Air rushes down into the lungs to fill the vacuum, filling the whole lungs-bottom to top. By pulling the belly in at the end of the exhalation, the process is reversed. The breath may be used as the focus of meditation. Since you can only breathe in the present moment an awareness of your breathing automatically puts you into the present moment.

Breathing Packet, Cont.

Breathing Exercises

Abdominal/Belly/Diaphragmatic Breathing

The Technique:

1. Place one hand on your chest and the other on your abdomen. When you take a deep breath in, the hand on the abdomen should rise higher than the one on the chest, insuring that the diaphragm is pulling air into the bases of the lungs.

2. After exhaling through the mouth, take a slow deep breath in through your nose. Take in as much air as you comfortably can. Hold it for a count of 7.

3. Slowly exhale through your mouth for a count of 8. As all the air is released with relaxation, gently contract your abdominal muscles to completely evacuate the remaining air from the lungs. It is important to remember that we deepen respirations not by inhaling more air, but through completely exhaling it.

4. Repeat the cycle four more times for a total of 5 deep breaths and try to breathe at a rate of one breath every 10 seconds (or 6 breaths per minute). At this rate our heart rate variability increases, which has a positive effect on cardiac health.

5. In general, exhalation should be twice as long as inhalation. The use of the hands on the chest and abdomen are only needed to help you train your breathing. Once you feel comfortable with your ability to breathe into the abdomen, they are no longer needed.

Alternate Nostril Breathing

With this exercise, we breathe through only one nostril at a time. The logic behind this exercise is that normal breathing does alternate from one nostril to the other at various times during the day. In a healthy person, the breath will alternate between nostrils about every two hours. According to the yogis, when the breath continues to flow in one nostril for more than two hours, as it does with most of us, it will have an adverse effect on our health. If the right nostril is involved, the result is mental and nervous disturbance. If the left nostril is involved, the result is chronic fatigue and reduced brain function. The longer the flow of breath in one nostril, the more serious the illness will be. Benefits: The exercise produces optimum function to both sides of the brain: that is optimum creativity and optimum logical verbal activity. This also creates a more balanced person, since both halves of the brain are functioning property. The yogis consider this to be the best technique to calm the mind and the nervous system.

The Technique:

1. Close the right nostril with your right thumb and inhale through the left nostril. Do this to the count of four seconds.

2. Immediately close the left nostril with your right ring finger and little finger, and at the same time remove your thumb from the right nostril, and exhale through this nostril. Do this to the count of eight seconds.

This completes a half round.

Breathing Packet, Cont.

3. Inhale through the right nostril to the count of four seconds.

4. Close the right nostril with your right thumb and exhale through the left nostril to the count of eight seconds.

This completes one full round.

5. Start by doing three rounds, adding one per week to seven rounds.

A Centering Breath

The Technique:

1. Begin by breathing slowly and gently all the way down, then pause and wait to breathe in again until your body initiates a breath. This will allow the O_2/CO_2 ratio in your body to rebalance.

2. Wait twenty or thirty seconds or longer before your body needs a breath. Don't wait so long that it feels uncomfortable. Just allow your body to tell you when it needs a breath, then gently let the air in and resume your regular breathing cycle.

3. After a few cycles of regular breathing, do a second Centering Breath.

4. Breathe slowly and gently all the way down, then pause and wait to breathe in again until your body tells you it needs a breath. When your body needs a breath, gently let the air in and resume your regular breathing cycle.

5. After a few cycles of regular breathing, do a third Centering Breath.

6. Breathe slowly and gently all the way down, then suspend the breath and wait to inhale until your body tells you it needs a breath. When your body needs a breath, gently let the air in and resume your regular breathing cycle.

The "C" Breath

The Technique:

Sit down with your feet flat on the floor, towards the front of the chair, so that only your pelvis rests on the chair.

1. Rest your hands on your lap.

2. Begin by inhaling and letting your stomach expand with your breath.

3. As your stomach expands slightly, let your pelvis roll forward and your spine extend while you bring your head up.

4. As you exhale, let your head drop down and your pelvis drop back. You'll find that your body makes a natural "C" shape.

5. Repeat the in-breath and the out-breath, allowing your breath to lead the movement.

6. On the inhale, relax the belly-muscles and let your spine flex so that your chin and head tilt up, at the same time rolling forward on your sit-bones.

7. On the exhale, roll back on to your sit-bones and tilt your chin/head down.

Breathing Packet, Cont.

The Stimulating Breath
Andrew Weil, M.D.

The Technique:

1. Inhale and exhale rapidly through your nose, keeping your mouth closed but relaxed. Inhalation and exhalation should be uniform in duration, but as short as possible.

2. Attempt three in-and-out breath cycles per second. This produces a quick movement of the diaphragm, suggesting a bellows.

3. Breathe normally after each cycle.

4. Do not do this for more than 15 seconds on your first try.

5. Each time you practice, you may increase your time by four or five seconds, until you reach a full minute.

The Relaxing Breath: 4–7–8 Exercise
Andrew Weil, M.D.

This exercise is calmative for the nervous system, activating the parasympathetic branch. Dr. Weil suggests that this be practiced at least twice a day, but do not do more than four breaths at one time for the first month of practice. It is an effective mechanism for combating internal stress and external stressors.

The Technique:

1. Sit in a chair with your back straight.

2. Place the tip of your tongue against the ridge of tissue just behind your upper front teeth, and keep it there throughout the breathing exercise.

3. Purse your lips slightly and exhale through your mouth around your tongue.

4. Exhale all the way out through your mouth, making a whoosh sound.

5. Close your mouth and inhale quietly through your nose to a count of four.

6. Hold your breath for a count of seven.

7. Exhale completely through your mouth, making a whoosh sound to a count of eight.

8. This is one breath cycle.

9. Now inhale again and repeat the breath cycle three more times for a total of four breaths.

Always inhale quietly through your nose and exhale audibly through your mouth. The tip of your tongue stays in position the whole time.

Exhalation takes twice as long as inhalation. The absolute time you spend on each phase is not important; the ratio of 4:7:8 is important. If you have trouble holding your breath, speed the exercise up, but keep to the ratio of 4:7:8 for the three phases.

BREATHING PACKET, CONT.

UJJAYI BREATH
"Ocean Sounding Breath"

The Ujjayi breath focuses the mind and generates internal heat. In Ujjai breathing, the glottis is partially closed. The glottis is that part in the throat area that closes when you swallow, but which is open when you breath. When you partially close the glottis while breathing, you can hear a sound resonate from within, as well as feel a flow of air on the palate. A slightly different sound is heard on inhalation and exhalation. During inhalation, tighten the abdominal muscles very slightly, and during exhalation the abdominal muscles are used to exhale completely.

The Technique:

1. Come into a comfortable seated position with your spine erect, or lie down on your back. Begin taking long, slow, and deep breaths through the nostrils.

2. Allow the breath to be gentle and relaxed as you slightly contract the back of your throat creating a steady hissing sound as you breathe in and out. The sound need not be forced, but it should be loud enough so that if someone came close to you they would hear it.

3. Lengthen the inhalation and the exhalation as much as possible without creating tension anywhere in your body, and allow the sound of the breath to be continuous and smooth.

4. To help create the proper "ah" sound, hold your hand up to your mouth and exhale as if trying to fog a mirror. Inhale the same way. Notice how you constrict the back of the throat to create the fog effect. Now close your mouth and do the same thing while breathing through the nose.

"COMPLETE" OR "THREE-PART" BREATH

The Technique:

1. Sit with your spine erect, or lie down on your back. Begin taking long, slow, and deep breaths through the nostrils.

2. As you inhale, allow the belly to fill with air, drawing air deep into the lower lungs.

3. As you exhale, allow the belly to deflate like a balloon.

4. Repeat several times, keeping the breath smooth and relaxed, and never straining.

5. Repeat several times.

6. Breathe into your belly as in step #1, but also expand the mid-chest region by allowing the rib cage to open outward to the sides.

7. Exhale and repeat several times.

8. Follow steps #1 and #2 and continue inhaling by opening the upper chest.

9. Exhale and repeat. Combining all three steps into one continuous or complete flow.

Breathing Packet, Cont.

Bellows Breath

The Technique:

1. Sit on the floor or in an armless chair with your spine straight.
2. Bend your elbows and make fists with your hands with the upper arms wrapped around the torso.
3. Take a normal natural breath in and out.
4. As you inhale through the nostrils, with some force raise your arms straight up as you open your palms to face outward, spreading your fingers wide.
5. Exhale strongly through the nose as you bring your arms back to the starting position, again making fists with your hands.
6. Do this at a moderate pace fifteen to twenty times.

Breath of Joy

The Technique:

1. Stand with your feet a comfortable distance apart and your arms at your sides.
2. Inhale one-third capacity through your nostrils and swing your arms up to shoulder level in front of you.
3. Inhale to two-thirds capacity and stretch your arms out to the sides.
4. Inhale to full capacity and swing your arms up over your head.
5. As you exhale through your mouth, lean forward and stretch your arms out to the sides and slightly behind you.
6. Repeat three to five times.

Breath of Awareness

This breathing is practiced with concentration placed on the midbrain in the very center of the head for cleansing and awareness.

The Technique:

1. Begin to inhale slowly, but sharply — breathing up toward the crown of the head, feeling the body lifting upward.
2. The inhalation should be made smoothly and continuously for as long as possible. At the peak of inhalation — when no more air can be taken in — quickly, but gently, release the breath downward toward the mouth.
3. Repeat several cycles noticing any changes in sensations as awareness moves from the lower centers to the higher self.

A BASIC BREATH MEDITATION
(Based on Sharon Salzberg & Joseph Goldstein's Insight Meditation)

According to Sharon Salzberg, mindfulness is one of the main pillars of meditation.

> . . . that means being aware of what is going on as it actually arises — not being lost in our conclusions or judgments about it; our fantasies of what it means; our hopes; our fears; our aversions. Rather, mindfulness helps us to see nakedly and directly; "this is what is happening right now." Through mindfulness, we pay attention to our pleasant experiences, our painful experiences, and our neutral experiences – the sum total of what life brings us.

The second pillar is concentration or

> . . . the development of stability of mind, a gathering in and focusing of our normal scattered energy. The state of concentration that we develop in meditative practice is tranquil, at ease, relaxed, open, yielding, gentle, and soft. We let things be; we don't try to hold on to experiences. This state is also alert — it's not about getting so tranquil that we just fall asleep. It's awake, present, and deeply connected with what is going on. This is the balance that we work with in developing concentration.

Therapist should read and record script. Give client a copy of the CD. Have the client play and follow the meditation twice daily. (For people with a history of sexual abuse please begin to practice in five minute intervals — increasing the duration as the client becomes more comfortable with the procedure.)

Client should begin by finding a quiet space where he/she will be undisturbed for the duration of the meditation. Take a comfortable posture sitting on a chair with your back supported and your feet comfortably on the floor.

Play script: "Close your eyes or find a spot a few feet in front of you to place your gaze. Begin to relax. Allow your mind to be spacious. Don't try to make anything happen, just begin to become aware of what is. Slowly bring your attention to the breath. Take a few deep breaths and release. Now allow your breath to return to normal — no need to control or change it in any way. Just notice the natural rhythm of the breath. Wherever you notice the breath most distinctly whether it be at the nostrils, the chest, or the abdomen, allow your attention to rest there.

As you feel the breath, you might silently label it — "in/out or rising and falling." As you feel the breath enter, noting "in" and as it leaves the body, "out."

Notice the cycle of the breath as it is appearing right now. Allow yourself to sustain attention through a full cycle. The beginning of the in breath — the end of the in breath, the pause, the beginning of the out breath through to the end of the out breath. Allow yourself to pay attention throughout an entire cycle.

You may find your mind wandering. That's fine. Our minds have been trained to be distracted. It doesn't matter. Each time you notice that you've lost touch with the breath simply notice and very gently bring your attention back . . . come back to the feeling of the breath in this very moment.

You may discover that there's a pause between the in breath and the out breath or between the out breath and the next breath. If you notice a pause, just allow your attention to settle there. Simply noticing what is; allowing the next breath to come naturally. There's nothing you need to do about it. There's no need to alter it or perfect it. Simply notice the breath as it arises.

Many distractions will appear — the mind will wander. It doesn't matter. When you practice you'll need to begin again and again. When you recognize that you've lost touch with

BREATHING PACKET, CONT.

an awareness of the breath . . . simply and lovingly return your attention to the breath as it is appearing right now. You can end this session by bringing your attention to your hands and feet. Slowly and gently opening your eyes.

INSIGHT MEDITATION KIT (CD)

". . . Insight Meditation makes it simple to start meditating in the Buddhist tradition. This elegant gift-boxed set includes two exclusive compact discs with authentic guided meditations, complemented by study cards and a special instruction book with the beginner in mind."

Sharon Salzberg, cofounder of the Insight Meditation Society & Joseph Goldstein's *Insight Meditation Kit* (CD), a comprehensive training course in basic meditation.

To Obtain Materials:

Website: http://store.soundstrue.com/aw00553.html

WALKING MEDITATION

This is a wonderful practice that can be done right in the middle of daily life, and *integrates* body, breath, and mind. You count internally with exhalation and inhalation, and align this with the steps you are taking while walking. So, for example, you may count 4:4. This means as you walk, you exhale while you internally count off 4 paces. At the end of this, you start to inhale, and count off 4 paces. You count 4 paces with exhalation, and 4 paces with inhalation. You literally speak the numbers as you count them, but only internally, silently in the mind.

Automatically, your breath becomes even. Automatically, your body and breath synchronize. Automatically, your mind synchronizes with the body and breath, by virtue of the internal counting. As you walk, you need to find the right pace that is comfortable, and in alignment with the speed you are walking. You might find that 2:2, 3:3, 4:4, 5:5, 6:6, etc., is the optimum speed for you.

As you get proficient with even breathing, you can shift to two-to-one breathing with walking, such as 6 paces with exhalation, and 3 paces with inhalation. Again, you need to find the pace that is comfortable for you. This practice can easily be done when you are walking even one or two minutes from one place to another. It brings great benefits, right in the middle of daily life, including a calm, peaceful mind and relaxation to the autonomic nervous system.

Exhale	Inhale	Ratio
4	4	1:1
3	3	1:1
5	4	1.25:1
4	3	1.33:1
6	4	1.5:1
3	2	1.5:1
8	4	2:1
6	3	2:1
2	1	2:1

Working Through Trauma: Energy Healing and Self-Soothing

According to the principles of energy medicine, a "skeleton" of energy supports the physical flesh and bones. The body's physical structure is built upon and animated by the energy body's structure of meridian pathways, chakra centers, aura, and other discrete energy systems. The energy structure is not just one big electromagnetic field. The variety of components in the energy "skeleton" mirrors the complexity of the physical body.

Anatomy of the Energy Body: The anatomical descriptions of the energy body are supported by electromagnetic measurements. They also correlate with descriptions of energy structures found throughout the world. Each culture has its own understanding and concepts related to the energy body.

The Meridians: a meridian carries energy in the same way that an artery transports blood. The meridian system functions as the body's energy bloodstream. It brings vitality and balance, removes blockages, adjusts metabolism, and determines the speed and form of cellular change. The meridian pathway's energy flow is as critical to the body as the flow of blood. There is no life without energy. Meridians affect all the organs and the physiological systems, including the immune, nervous, endocrine, circulatory, respiratory, digestive, skeletal, muscular, and lymphatic systems. Each system is fed by at least one meridian. Blocked or unregulated energy flow through a meridian will have a negative effect on the system that the meridian feeds. The meridians include fourteen channels that transport energy into and throughout the body. The meridian pathways also link hundreds of tiny, discrete reservoirs of heat and electromagnetic energy along the surface of the skin. The reservoirs are acupuncture points. When these points are stimulated with needles or physical pressure, energy is released and redistributed along the meridian pathway.

Thought Field Therapy (TFT)

Developed by psychologist Roger Callahan, Thought Field Therapy (TFT) can be described as psychological acupressure. It builds upon a foundation of elements from EMDR and introduces a new technique, tapping. The client taps on specific acupressure points while focusing on the traumatic material. The tapping technique is inspired by concepts of Chinese energy medicine that are widely accepted in holistic health circles. Within this conceptual framework, physical and emotional problems result when the body's energy is blocked. In TFT, the therapist directs the client to tap gently on critical acupressure points along the body's energy meridians. This tapping helps the body's energy to flow and rebalance.

EMOTIONAL FREEDOM TECHNIQUE (EFT)

EFT is a less expensive variation of TFT. It too has been described as a needle-less acupuncture for the emotions. In addition to the simpler, all-purpose tapping protocol, EFT also instructs people to speak affirmations and engage in unusual, yet seemingly effective behaviors, including tapping, eye movements, humming, and counting. Gary Craig, a student of Roger Callahan, developed EFT, by combining EMDR's eye movements and emphasis on shifting underlying cognitive belief systems with a more generalized acupressure point tapping, based on TFT. Seems he threw in a few additional distraction techniques just for laughs. One cycle of EFT takes only a few minutes, generates little distress and it can be effective even if the client does not believe that it would be.

There have been no formal research studies done to empirically prove efficacy of these acupressure techniques. However, clinicians and clients alike seem impressed with the results that they've been getting (author included). According to van der Kolk, et al (1996), effective treatment requires exposure to, without total re-experiencing of, the traumatic material; too much arousal precludes assimilation of any new information. It may be that the tapping protocol in TFT and EFT provides a concrete physical stimulus drawing attention back to the here and now, anchoring clients in the present. It also appears that the physical, rhythmic stimulation has a calming and soothing effect on agitated clients. This is most likely produced by the reciprocal inhibitory relaxation response of the parasympathetic nervous system's reducing the effects of the hyperactivated sympathetic nervous system. (Carbonell and Figley, 1995)

In EFT, you tap gently on certain acupuncture meridians on the face and the body as you tune into the problem you want to resolve. The tapping process, combined with your focused attention on the issue you want to resolve, can reduce physical and emotional pains, end cravings/habits, and relieve anxiety, fears and phobias, sometimes with remarkable speed and often with long-lasting positive effects.

> *I know what you're thinking: There's no way my clients will go for this! I had that thought too. I was right in some cases; some folks are never going to try it. But most will, especially when you do it with them and ask them to humor you. If it takes away their distress quickly, they will use it. People do what works — especially if it works fast, which EFT does.*

CLIENT HANDOUT:
THE EFT "BASIC RECIPE"

How long does it take to learn?
Usually one can learn the basic recipe within a few minutes. Once familiar with this process, you can do the whole round in less than 2 minutes.

Before You Begin: Identify the specific problem and observe how it feels: thoughts, sensations, and emotions that are associated with the issue. Using a SUDS (Subjective Units of Distress Scale) rate your distress from 0– 10 (0=no distress, 10= the worst distress you can imagine)

Follow four components "Basic Recipe"

1. **The Setup**

   Start your EFT process by tapping firmly on your Karate Chop point.

   Setup Phrase: Next, bring up the negative emotion and/or problem you want to address.

   Note the SUDS level from 0 to 10 (0=none 10=worst). Then say the following statement three times and with conviction, aloud if possible (though not necessary), as you firmly tap on the Karate Chop point:

   "Even though I have this _____, I clearly and completely accept myself." (Fill the blank with the negative emotion or issue you want to address.) For example: *"Even though I have this craving for chocolate, I deeply and completely accept myself"* or *"Even though I feel so angry at him, I deeply and completely accept myself."*

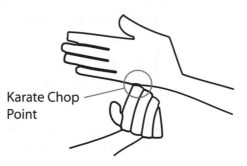

Karate Chop Point

First point: Karate Chop (KC).

- It's on the center of the fleshy part of the outside of either hand.
- Firmly tap the Karate Chop point with the combined flattened fingers from the other hand.
- Tap softly but firmly and not to hurt or bruise yourself in the process.

2. **The Sequence**

   Once the setup step is complete, place your index finger and middle finger together. Using the tips of these fingers, tap about seven times on each of the following meridian points. Tap firmly, but not so hard that you bruise or hurt yourself. (Most of the tapping points exist on either side of the body. It doesn't matter whether you tap on the right side or the left, nor does it matter if you switch sides during the Sequence. For example, you can tap under your right eye and, later in the Sequence, tap under your left arm.) As you tap on these points, it is necessary to keep your mind tuned to the issue you are resolving with EFT. To do that, say a *Reminder Phrase:* "This _____ *(issue)"* as you tap on each of the points. Using the above example for the problem of chocolate craving, the *Reminder Phrase* would be "This craving for chocolate."

Here are the tapping points *(see illustration on next page):*

Going down the face and the body, tap on the following points as you say your *Reminder Phrase,* "This _____ *(issue),"* starting from:

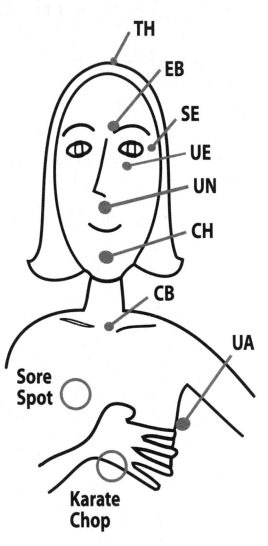

1. **EB** = beginning of the Eye Brow (on either the left or right one.)

2. **SE** = Side of your Eye (of either left or right eye, tap on the boney part of the eye socket right at the corner of your eye. Don't get too close to the eye that you hurt yourself, but don't go too far off that you are tapping on your temple.)

3. **UE** = Under the Eye (of either left or right eye, again on the boney part of the eye socket, about 1 inch straight under the pupil.)

4. **UN** = Under the Nose (roughly midway under the bottom of the nose and the top of the lip).

5. **CH** = Chin (midway between chin and the bottom of lower lip).

6. **CB** = Beginning of the Collar Bone (where the breastbone, collarbone, and first rib meet).

7. **UA** = Under the Arm (about 4 inches below your arm pit on either left or right side of your body).

8. **TH** = Top of the Head

3. **The 9 Gamut Procedures**

After completing the Sequence, you are now ready to carry out "The 9-Gamut Procedure." This procedure fine-tunes the brain via eye movements, humming, and counting so as to enhance the effects of the tapping. It tunes the brain to the right frequency for the problem. Through connecting nerves, certain parts of the brain are stimulated when eyes are moved. Likewise, the right side of the brain is engaged when you hum a song and the left side is engaged when you count.

During this procedure, nine of these brain-stimulating actions are performed while simultaneously and continuously tapping "the Gamut Point." While continually tapping on the Gamut Point, carry out all the following:

9 Brain-Balancing steps

1. Close your eyes

2. Open your eyes

3. Eyes hard down right while holding the head steady (stimulates kinesthetic sensations and memory)

4. Eyes hard down left while holding the head steady (internal dialogue)

5. Roll the eyes in a circle clockwise (stimulates visual and auditory memory and imagination)

6. Roll the eyes counter-clockwise (as above)

7. Hum "Happy Birthday", or any song, for 2 bars (this engages the right brain)

8. Count to 5 (this engages the left brain)

9. Hum "Happy Birthday", or any song, for 2 bars again (this engages the right brain)

The Sequence again:

After completing "The 9-Gamut Procedure," repeat the Sequence. That's it. Now you have the basic recipe for EFT!

Take a Deep Breath, Check-In, and Reassess:

After each round of EFT, take a deep breath in, and gently breathe out. Take a moment to check in with yourself. Notice how you are feeling now, physically and emotionally; notice what thoughts, memories, or emotions are up for you. Without judging yourself right or wrong, just observe.

Next, reassess the intensity level of the problem. What is the intensity level now? If you are at a 0, you are done. Congratulations! If not, you may need to do one or more subsequent rounds until you feel the intensity has gone down to 0.

(Gary Craig is the founder of EFT and the host of the web site www.emofree.com. "Best of all, anyone can learn and use EFT and you don't need specialized schooling for it. We even give away the basic methods as a free download.")

CLIENT HANDOUT: ACUPRESSURE POINTS (NEEDLE-LESS ACUPUNCTURE)

Relief of Anxiety and Panic
Press CV 17

Anxiety and panic can cause us to hold our breath or hyperventilate. Neither condition is particularly desirable. So, when this occurs, begin by pressing the Sea of Tranquility point, which is located four finger-widths above the base of the breastbone, at the level of the heart. Press into the indentations with your middle three fingers. Breathing slowly through your nose, begin to relax as you focus solely on your breath for next two minutes.

Special Points for Relieving Traumatic Stress

1. **Letting Go (Lu 1)**

   These two emotional healing points are located on the outer sides of the chest, four finger-widths up from the armpit crease and one finger-width inward. Cross your arms over the chest center. Place your fingertips firmly on both sides of your outer chest. Breathe deeply and hold these points for about two minutes.

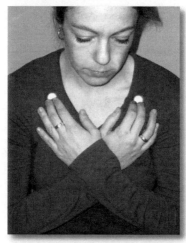

2. **Gates of Consciousness (GB 20)**

   These two points are located about three inches apart. Place the thumbs just below the base of the skull, in the hollow between the two large neck muscles.

   With your thumbs, press underneath the base of the skull into the indentations on both sides. Close your eyes and slowly tilt your head back. Visualize this mental balancing point relieving your panic and anxiety as you gently press up underneath your skull for one to two minutes. Take slow, deep breaths. These points help relieve headaches, neck stiffness and pain, trauma, shock hypertension, and irritability.

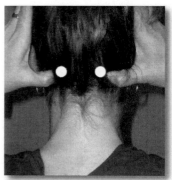

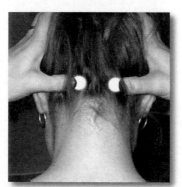

3. Third Eye (GV 24.5)

This point is between the eyebrows, in the indentation between the nose bridge and the forehead. To activate this point, sit up with a straight back. Close your eyes and tilt your chin down slightly. Bring your palms together and up to your forehead. Lightly touch the Third Eye point with the tips of your middle and index fingers. Breathe slowly and deeply for one minute.

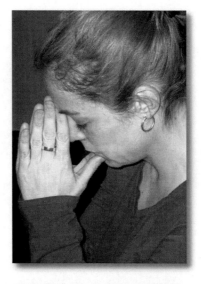

Clear Mind (GB 14)

These emotional balancing points are located one finger-width above the eyebrows, in line with the center of the iris. Lightly place the thumb above one eye and the third finger above the other eye

Anxiety Reduction
Inner Gate (P6)

This point is three finger-widths away from the center of the crease inside the wrist. Place the right thumb on the point on the left arm. Wrap your fingertips around the outside of the arm and place them directly behind your thumb. Firmly grasp the arm and hold for one minute. Breathe deeply. Switch wrists and hold for another minute.

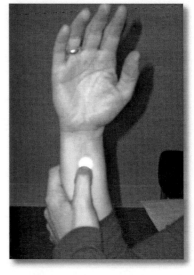

Acupressure Points, Cont.

Balancing Emotions and Soothing Anxiety
Sea of Tranquility (CV 17)

This point is on the center of the breastbone, four finger-widths up from the base of the sternum. Gently press this point with the middle three fingertips. At the same time, concentrate as you take deep, slow breaths into your heart for three minutes.

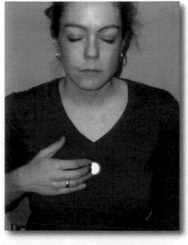

Interrupt a Panic Attack (P 9)

This point is located at the base of the middle fingernail. Hold this point firmly against the thumb of the same hand. Take long, slow, deep breaths for three minutes.

Prevent Dissociation/ Re-Association (GV 26)

This point is in the middle of the upper lip, two-thirds of the way up towards the nose. Using your index or middle fingertip, press firmly on GV 26. Place your finger so that you angle some pressure into the upper gum. Breathe deeply and hold for two minutes

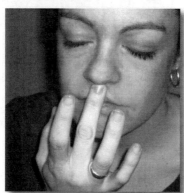

Promotion of Security and Affect Regulation
Step 1— Press Lu 1

Roll a towel firmly and position it between your shoulder blades as you lay down. Cross your wrists over the center of your chest. Place your fingertips on the Letting Go point (Lu 1), which are the two points on the upper, outer part of the chest. Rub your chest muscles, find the tightest spot and place your middle fingertips on that spot. Adjust a towel between the shoulder blades so that it applies firm, but comfortable pressure on the upper back. Keep firm

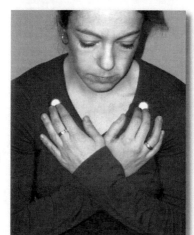

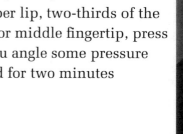

ACUPRESSURE POINTS, CONT.

pressure on the Letting Go points as you concentrate on breathing deeply for one to three minutes.

Step 2 — Press GB 20

Position your thumbs underneath the base of your skull, in the indentations that are three inches apart. With your eyes closed, slowly tilt your head back as you gradually press up and under the skull. Inhale and exhale slowly and deeply as you direct the pressure firmly upward and inward. (GB 20). Relax and breathe deeply as you hold GB 20 for one to three minutes or until you feel a regular, even pulse on both sides. Continue to breathe into your emotions as you slowly release the pressure.

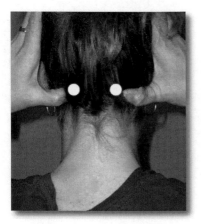

Acupressure Points for Healing Sexual Trauma

The following three poses address physical and psychological issues, employing acupressure points that are connected with certain vital energy centers, or charkas, to heal trauma associated with sexual abuse.

Step 1 — Hold CV 6

Locate the point two finger-widths directly below the navel. Place the fingertips of both hands directly on the point between your navel and your pubic bone. With steady pressure, gradually press in about an inch. Maintain steady, firm pressure as you breathe deeply. If you are comfortable enough to close your eyes, do so. If not, find a spot on which to focus approximately eighteen inches in front of you. Imagine yourself in a safe place, feeling contained protected and supported. Let your body relax and sink into the ground.

Step 2 — Hold SP 16

Locate SP 16, which are the two points at the base of your ribcage, directly under your nipples. Curve your fingertips in as your press on SP 16. Apply gentle upward pressure into the slight indentations for two minutes. Breathe deeply into your core.

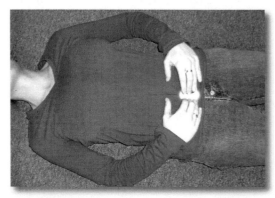

Step 3 — Hold SP 12 and SP 13

Take all of your fingertips and locate the ropy ligament in the center of the leg crease at the top of each thigh. Using moderate pressure, hold for one minute. Feel for a strong pulse from the large artery that runs through these points. Breathe deeply into your core.

Working Through Trauma: Somatic Exercises

(Based on the work of Peter Levine)

Grounding and Centering

Initial Instructions

1. Begin to discover your center of gravity by standing in a stable way.

2. Sense your feet on the ground. Paying attention to the way that they make contact with the ground.

3. With your feet firmly on the ground, slowly begin to move — swaying slowly from side to side, then forward and backwards.

4. Notice the feelings in your body as you move.

5. Place your hands below your navel and breathe in and out while continuing to sway.

6. Settle.

7. Now sit in a chair with your feet on the floor.

8. Once again, place your hands below your navel and sense the energy coming into that area through your feet.

Flight Exercise: The Great Escape

This scenario below should be discussed/developed by the client and therapist. It should be individualized for the client, being mindful of past history as well as client's strengths and vulnerabilities. As always, safety is of the utmost importance.

1. Instruct the client to sit in a chair with a firm cushion/pillow under his/her feet.

2. Instruct the client to settle into the chair, feeling his/her feet on the cushion.

3. Have the client bring his/her awareness to all of the places where his/her body makes contact with the chair and the cushion.

4. Instruct the client to close his/her eyes and imagine walking down a street, when suddenly a rabid dog springs from a fenced in yard and begins chasing the client.

5. Instruct the client to begin his/her escape with ease.

6. Have the client pay attention to his/her lower body strength as (s)he moves his/her legs up and down in an exaggerated running motion.

7. Continue to instruct the client to remain mindful of his/her legs and body as (s)he continues to run on the pillow.

8. Instruct the client to run until (s)he has escaped from the dog and reached safety.

9. Have the client announce when (s)he has made it to safety, then instruct client to sit, rest and allow himself/herself to settle-paying attention to breathing and heartbeat and any other bodily sensations.

The following two exercises will help toward the reestablishment of feelings of strength, healthy aggression, and empowerment. This technique requires two people: the pusher (client) and the pushed (therapist)

PUSH HANDS!

1. Client places the palms of his/her hands comfortably against the palm of the therapist's hands.

2. The therapist instructs the client to become aware of the feeling of strength and force arising from her/his center.

3. The therapist instructs the client to slowly exert pressure on the therapist's hands.

4. Instruct to push as far as she/he wants while keeping his/her balance.

5. The therapist's job is simply to be there and to provide the resistance necessary to meet the pressure by mirroring the client's strength.

6. If the therapist senses that the client is collapsing or backing off, modulate the degree of eye contact until they have regained their strength.

Figure 8: Push Hands

7. Decrease resistance slightly from time to time to determine if the pusher is maintaining his or her balance.

EMPOWERMENT/HEALTHY AGGRESSION

PUSH BACK!

1. Therapist and client begin by standing back to back. Leaning up against one another, while maintaining the feeling of being grounded.

2. Feel the inner support in your upper and lower back.

3. Instruct the client to notice and report any bodily sensations.

4. Instruct the client to just allow the experience. Taking notice of any shaking and/or trembling while leaning into this support of the therapist's back.

5. Once settled, instruct the client to slowly begin to push against the therapist's back.

6. The therapist's job is simply to be there and to provide the resistance necessary to meet the pressure by mirroring the client's strength.

7. Therapist should instruct the client to notice the feeling of power coming from her/his legs and center.

Figure 9: Push Back

Experiments from the Center for Somatic Studies

The purpose of each of these graduated experiments is to highlight supports for contacting — basic coordinated movements that enable an individual to be in touch with oneself and the environment. In patterns that result from trauma, these supports are often insufficient in their availability to create ongoing spontaneous connections. The individual lives out of touch with his body and the world. Enlivening basic coordinated supports that underlie and accompany contact allows the person to more easily contain and modulate experience and its expression. This is crucial in working with and through historic and traumatic events.

— Ruella Frank, Ph.D.

First Sequence: Finding Ground (tennis ball required)

Stand with your feet hip-width apart and pointed in the forward direction. Notice how much of each foot rests upon the floor and to what extent you experience the floor coming up to meet each foot? Now, take a tennis ball and roll it under one foot, carefully pressing each part of the foot onto the ball — your heel, toes, and the ball of your foot. To the degree that you hold tension in your feet is the degree that you will feel some discomfort. After you have finished rolling the ball underneath your foot, stand upright and pay attention to the difference (if any) between the foot that has rolled onto the tennis ball and the one that has not. After carefully considering differences between the two, the tennis ball is used on the other foot. When this is done, both feet are placed on the floor and compared another time.

The experiment is diagnostic and therapeutic. The person learns how much he or she rests upon the earth and feels supported by it. The tennis ball creates a kinetic chain that thrusts upward from the sole of the foot through the leg, thigh, into the hip socket and continues upward through the spine. Tight muscles of foot and leg are released, so one can better experience the bones of the foot pressing downward while the floor is also experienced as pressing upward to meet each foot.

Sequence Two: Feeling One's Weight

Sit in a chair with your feet hip-width apart, planted on the floor and pointed in the forward direction. Rest your spine onto the back of the chair. If it is not possible to have your feet on the floor while maintaining your spine against the chair's back, a towel can be neatly rolled and placed the length of your spine to create support along the back-body. Place both hands along your thighs, fingers in the forward facing direction and palms down. Notice how the weight of your body — your spine, pelvis, and backs of your legs — rests on the chair. Notice the weight of your feet on the floor.

Now lift one foot about two inches off the floor and then release it downward so that it drops onto the floor. Repeat this with the other foot. The movement is done several times and alternating the feet — lift/drop, lift/drop, lift/drop. Next, do a similar movement with each hand on your thigh — lift/drop, lift/drop, lift/drop. Once again, pay attention to the weight of your body on the chair, your hands on your lap, and your feet on the floor and compare it with the earlier experience.

We only experience ourselves through an experience of our body weight. Our weight informs us that we are here, how we are here, and where we are in space. The lift-dropping of feet and hands enhances the experience of body-weight and offers greater clarity in the capacity to orient.

SEQUENCE THREE: BEING PRESENT

Sit in a chair, spine well-supported, and both feet pointing forward and planted on the floor. Feel the back of your body, pelvis and thighs resting onto the chair and your feet on the floor. Take one hand and place it over your breastbone. Breathe easily and notice where your hand meets your heart — or the area just under your breastbone. Sense your hand as it moves with your breathing. Feeling hand over heart and the movement of your breath, say aloud, "Right now, I am here." Aware of one hand placed over the heart (or one hand resting on another) creates a subtle resistance. The pressure between one part of the body and another organizes the experience of coherence — "This is where I come together." Language is added to complete the process.

Ruella Frank, Ph.D., has been exploring early infant movements and their relationship to the adult since the mid-1970s. She brings many years of experience to her work as a Gestalt psychotherapist — as a professional dancer, yoga practitioner/teacher, student of the concepts of Body/Mind Centering, and student of Laura Perls, co-founder of Gestalt therapy. Ruella is director of the Center for Somatic Studies, faculty at Gestalt Associates for Psychotherapy and the New York Institute for Gestalt Therapy, and also teaches throughout the United States and the world. She is author of articles and chapters in various publications, as well as the book Body of Awareness: A Somatic and Developmental Approach to Psychotherapy, is now available in four languages.

WORKING THROUGH TRAUMA: YOGA

If you want to use yoga to heal emotional pain, you must find out where it resides in your body and learn to take your breath there. I don't teach yoga to help people to transcend. I want people's spirits to reside in their body. I literally want to help people embody their spirit. Not go through life fragmented.

— Ana Forrest

Yoga cultivates your witness consciousness. It allows you to observe yourself on the mat. You aren't numbing out or going into default mode by overworking, watching TV, or reaching for the alcohol or carbs. For a trauma survivor, yoga, when practiced with awareness of breath and sensation, can be a gentle way to begin to reoccupy her body. When living in a body feels safe again, yoga postures can be used therapeutically to hold and then release the trauma stored there. Often the emotional and physical releases happen without reference to the story, so the survivor is no longer trapped in the victim role.

—Amy Weintraub

THE THEORY

The effects of trauma are primarily physiological — leaving an indelible biological imprint. Trauma disrupts clients' relationships to their bodies and emotions, leaving them feeling constricted, tense, helpless, disconnected, hurt, agitated, frantic, and in conflict with themselves, others and the world. Addressing the body's deep sensations and emotions, Hatha Yoga facilitates clients in; addressing their autonomic nervous system symptoms of hyperarousal; processing their traumatic memories; promoting mastery over the posttraumatic legacy of self-doubt and despair; appreciably changing how they organize themselves in relation to the world; and aiding in the reclamation of autonomy and authority over their own lives.

The Trauma Center at Justice Resource Institute (JRI) in Massachusetts (http://www. traumacenter.org) has conducted preliminary research investigating Hatha Yoga's effect on some common symptomatology of PTSD. The research bears out yoga's efficacy on core physiology associated with PTSD including Heart Rate Variability (HRV).

Although there are different types of yoga, most Westerners already identify yoga with Hatha Yoga — a yoga that seeks to promote health and well-being through physical exercise. With its profound effect on the circulation and on the functioning of the inner organs, glands, and nerves, a regular practice of asanas (postures), and breathing exercises (pranayama) makes the physical body strong, supple, and healthy. In addition, yoga offers psychological and spiritual benefits as well.

Psychological benefits include stress reduction and a general sense of well-being. Spiritually, a yoga practice can counter the sense of isolation often experienced by trauma clients, offering, instead a sense of connection to the Divine Being or a feeling of transcendence. Yoga is the one single technique that combines and provides the benefits of breathing exercises, stretching, fitness programs and meditation. Because it is a system for restoring balance to the body, mind and spirit, Yoga is an ideal modality for trauma clients. By working with the body and the breath in a series of postures (asanas), yoga enables them to release muscle tension, gain flexibility and strength, and quiet the mind.

Amy Weintraub: http://www.yogafordepression.com/index.html
Book: *Yoga for Depression: A Compassionate Guide to Relieve Suffering Through Yoga.* (Broadway Books, 2004).

Working Through Trauma:
Progressive Muscle Relaxation

Progressive Muscle Relaxation (PMR) is a relaxation technique that is simple and easy to learn. The PMR procedure teaches clients to relax muscles through a two-step process. First the client deliberately applies tension to certain muscle groups. The next step is to release the tension and turn the attention and awareness to the muscles as the tension flows away.

Through repetitive practice, clients quickly learn to recognize—and distinguish—the associated feelings of a tensed muscle and a relaxed muscle. With this simple knowledge, clients can then induce physical muscular relaxation at the first signs of the tension that accompanies anxiety. It is physically impossible for the body to simultaneously experience the anxiety response AND the relaxation response. With physical relaxation comes some degree of mental calmness—in any situation.

A Simple, Progressive Muscle Relaxation

The therapist reads and records the script and then gives the client an audio CD of the recording with instructions to play and follow muscle relaxation in the evening. It is very important that the client and therapist experiment with this exercise in session, and then decide whether this practice is appropriate. (Some clients begin to experience intense anxiety with this exercise — truly not what the creators had in mind in the way of client outcomes.)

Recommendations:

Having the therapist's voice on the client's CD both soothes and serves as a transition object for client.

- To induce meditative state and enhance the experience, add alpha wave medita tion music as background for the script.

Instructions:

If you are sitting in a chair, first move down to the floor. Next, sit up straight with your legs stretched out in front of you. From this sitting position, gently lower your body down until you are lying on your back, on the ground. Your legs are stretched out straight in front of you, arms resting at your sides. From this position, you will begin a sequence of tensing and relaxing each of your hands, feet, shoulders, and buttocks. Follow the steps in the sequence given:

1. Begin by tensing all the muscles in your face. Make a tight grimace, close your eyes as tightly as possible, clench your teeth, even move your ears up if you can. Hold this for the count of eight as you inhale.

2. Now exhale and relax completely. Let your face go completely lax, as though you were sleeping. Feel the tension seep from your facial muscles, and enjoy the feeling.

3. Next, completely tense your neck and shoulders, again inhaling and counting to eight. Then exhale and relax.

4. Continue down the body, repeating the procedure with the following muscle groups:

   • chest

   • abdomen

   • entire right arm

   • right forearm and hand (making a fist)

   • right hand

   • entire left arm

   • left forearm and hand (again, making a fist)

   • left hand

   • buttocks

   • entire right leg

   • lower right leg and foot

   • right foot

   • entire left leg

   • lower left leg and foot

   • left foot

The Short Version:

While keeping the rest of your body relaxed, make a fist with your right hand only, squeeze it for a count of five and let it relax. Repeat this movement with your left hand.

Point your right foot for a count of five, keeping the rest of your body relaxed, and then flex it for a count of five. Relax the right foot and repeat this movement with your left foot.

Clench your buttocks for a count of five and release them. After your buttocks, shrug your shoulders up to your ears for a count of five, and then relax them back to your resting position.

Now, it is time to breathe. Concentrate on your breath as you draw it in through your nose, and exhale it gently out of your mouth. Remain in this position for about ten breaths. If thoughts begin to crowd into your mind, bring your attention back, concentrating only the action of the breath.

Working Through Trauma: Guided Imagery

According to Belleruth Naparstek, Guided imagery is intentional, directed daydreaming-blending one's imagination with words and phrases that evoke sensory fantasy and memory. Guided imagery creates a deeply receptive mind, body, psyche and spirit state during which change becomes possible. For most of us, imagery is an accessible form of meditation yielding immediate empirically proven benefits including a wide variety of physical and psychological outcomes. The ones of interest to this population include:

- Reduction of anxiety and depression
- Decrease in blood pressure
- Strengthening of immune function
- Reduction of pain
- Reduction of bingeing and purging in those with bulimia
- Improvement in attention and concentration

Imagery is effective because it basically bypasses rational thought and logical assumptions — delivering healing messages directly to the hypervigilant primitive brain. Once received, imagery disperses gentle reminders of health, strength, meaning, and hope that affect unconscious assumptions and self-defeating concepts.

Because it is processed through the right brain's primitive, sensory, and emotion-based channels, it is an ideal intervention for post-traumatic stress. Imagery works on the right brain the home of feeling, sensing, and perceiving, rather than the thinking, judging, analyzing and deciding functions of the left-brain. Since it does not depend on the brain's logical and analytic centers, it circumvents psychological resistance, fear, hopelessness, worry, and doubt, and goes directly to attitude and self-esteem, without interference from the rather obstinate, literal mind.

Brain development studies have shown that a traumatized brain is no longer able to focus on language or verbal content. Instead, it spends all its time processing nonverbal danger cues—body movements, facial expressions, and tone of voice—as it searches for information about danger and threat. The primitive brain in effect co-opts cognition and behavior in the service of safety and survival. Unfortunately, this causes a distinct loss in ability to think abstractly, process language, and attend to ideas or word meanings. These functions are higher cortical functions — gray matter issues — that can only be attended to once the primitive brain is sufficiently calmed. It seems clear that interventions that rely on cognitive, problem-solving activities do not, and more importantly, cannot have much impact on these clients or their terror-driven behavior.

With the advancement of technology, neuroscience has shown us that traumatic changes appear in Broca's area of the brain, where personal experience gets translated into language. It appears that survivors can see, hear, smell, taste, and feel parts of the traumatic event, yet struggle unsuccessfully to translate these sensory elements into language. In addition to this "speechless terror," some long-term trauma survivors experience an additional obstacle in their analytic ability. Due to persistently high elevation of stress hormones, causing a reduction in the size of the hippocampus, survivors are often less able to put things in context and/or make critical distinctions about what is and what is not threatening in the present. Without this necessary discernment, survivors become more and more impulsive and less and less inhibited. In effect, what survivors are left with is a constantly hyper-aroused autonomic nervous system; an inability to distinguish past from present threat — necessarily producing a state of constant hypervigilance; a speechless terror accompanied by painful and traumatic sensory and body memories; and a marked inability to access any of their own cognitive resources.

Quite a predicament.

What should be resoundingly apparent to the reader is that talking "about trauma" — which requires participation from the language/logic portion of the left brain — is inadequate, oftentimes triggering, and very likely re-traumatizing to the client. A better option for therapists would be to target the client's highly sensitive, hyperacute right hemisphere with its over functioning visual, sensory, and emotional channels. By accessing the limbic system and the right hemisphere of the brain, survivors are able to process the images, body sensations, and feelings, attach some sort of meaning to them, and eventually move toward a more helpful and adaptive resolution of the traumatic material.

Imagery seems to offer a viable solution. Using a calming tone of voice, music, and symbolic representations of safety, imagery quiets the hypervigilant primitive brain, creating an environment where the higher brain can once again function in the service of the survivor.

Naparstek posits that guided imagery provides a cushion of evocative, multisensory protective images and built-in emotional safety. Appealing memories and lush fantasies require little energy or discipline to evoke. They provide distraction from pain; carry clients beyond worry, fear, and anguish she goes on to report that guided imagery has the ability to avoid the direct traps of language and literalism. A powerful healing tool, that provides a kinder, gentler and more effective route to tending to wounds of the inner self. Naparstek explains that the imaginary world developed through imagery is a generous place where clients can gain distance by locking pain away in a safe, floating it away on the wind, or erasing it from an imaginary blackboard. In this world, clients can summon protection and support from magical allies, remembered friends, favorite animals, powerful ancestors, guardian angels, and other divine helpers. They can create as many layers of distance between the traumatic event and themselves as needed. All the while surrounding themselves with loving, powerful protectors. (Naparstek, 2006)

Therapist should read and record script. Give client a copy of the CD. Have the client play and follow muscle relaxation in the evening. It is very important that the client and therapist experiment with this exercise in session, and then decide whether this practice is appropriate. (Some clients begin to experience intense anxiety with this exercise-truly not what the creators had in mind in the way of outcomes.)

- Having the therapist's voice on the client's CD allows for soothing in addition to serving as a transition object for client.
- To induce meditative state and enhance the experience, add alpha wave meditation music as background for the script.

(For information on Alpha Wave Meditation *see: Brainwave Suite* by Jeffrey Thompson http://www.healingproducts.com/relaxationcompany.htm)

THE PROTECTOR SCRIPT

Please begin by making yourself comfortable, shifting your weight so you're feeling well supported . . . (pause) . . . and gently allowing your eyes to close . . . Letting your hands rest comfortably somewhere on your body . . . on your chest, midriff or abdomen . . . so you can feel the rise of your body when you breathe in . . . and the way it settles back down when you breathe out . . . and you're becoming more and more attuned to your breath, as it moves in and out of your body . . . Inhaling deeply and slowly, all the way down into your belly . . . (pause) . . . and breathing out, fully and completely . . . feeling the expansion of your abdomen with each in-breath . . . and the way it subsides with each out-breath . . . And again, breathing in . . . and this time, imagining that you're sending the warm energy of your breath to any part of your body that's sore or tense or tight . . . (pause) . . . and releasing the tension with the exhale . . . so you can feel your breath going to all the tight, tense places . . . warming and loosening and softening them . . . and then, gathering up all the tension . . . and breathing it out . . . so that more and more, you can feel safe and comfortable, relaxed and easy . . . noticing your breath . . . with friendly but detached awareness . . . And as you continue to breathe in and out . . . deeply and easily . . . and you might begin to notice a tingling in the air all around you . . . the pleasant, subtle feel of energy on your skin . . . tingling and vibrating . . .as if you were surrounded and protected by a magical cushion of air . . . alive with humming energy . . . tingly waves of it, sparkling and dancing with light and color . . . becoming fuller, denser, with every breath . . . a force field of protection and safety . . . softly pulsing around you . . . gently insulating you from anything you don't want or need . . .

And now, sensing this cushion of energy drawing to it all the love and sweetness that has ever been felt for you by anyone at any time . . . pulling in all the caring, all the loving kindness that has ever been sent your way . . . every prayer and good wish . . . permeating and filling the field of energy around you . . . every smile, every nod of respect . . . every thank you and gesture of gratitude . . . pulling it all in like a powerful magnet . . . calling every good wish home . . . and so increasing the powerful, protective field all around you . . . And perhaps even sensing around you . . . the presence of those who've loved and nurtured you . . . or those who love you now . . . or who will love you in the future . . . just the ones you want with you . . . and sensing them around you now . . . maybe catching a fleeting glimpse of somebody . . . or noticing an old, familiar scent . . . or hearing the timbre of a dearly loved voice . . . possibly feeling a presence by your side . . . or the soft weight of a gentle hand on your shoulder. People from your life . . . alive or long gone . . . there might even be a special animal . . .a powerful ancestor . . . a guardian angel . . . sweet spirits or magical beings . . . special helpers and healers . . . allies, teachers, and guides . . . all come to lend assistance . . . invoked by your intention to heal, fully and completely . . . and some might be familiar and some not . . . and it doesn't matter . . . just so you feel their protection and support . . . breathing it into your heart . . . letting it fill you . . . Breathing in all that love and care, fully and deeply . . . all the way into your heart . . . filling up with it . . . feeling its warmth spread all through your body . . . gently pulsing out from the center of your heart . . . and diffusing through your body . . . spreading widely and evenly, like ripples in a pond . . . So you can feel a peaceful calm and balance settle over you . . . evening you out . . . filling you with a nourishing softness . . . as your heart becomes more and more peaceful . . . steady and calm . . . Breathing in the protection all around you . . . knowing it is always there . . . yours to notice, whenever you wish . . . And so . . . whenever you are ready . . . taking another full, deep breath . . . and gently, with soft eyes, coming back into the room whenever you are ready . . . knowing in a deep place that you are better for this . . .

And so you are . . .

For further information about Belleruth's work or to order CDs, please visit: http://www.healthjourneys.com/

- *Staying Well with Guided Imagery*, (Warner Books)
- *Your Sixth Sense*, (Harper San Francisco)
- *Invisible Heroes: Survivors of Trauma and How They Heal*

BODY MIND APPRECIATION EXERCISE

Deb Shapiro has trained extensively in various schools of bodywork, Buddhist meditation, and Jungian psychology in both England and America. She has been teaching both body-mind therapy and meditation with her husband, Ed Shapiro, for the past 20 years. Her books include The Body Mind Workbook (Vega Books, 2002), Meditation: Four Steps to Calmness and Clarity (Vega Books, 2003), and Unconditional Love (Time Warner AOL 2003). She and Ed reside in Boulder, Colorado. For further information, visit: www.edanddebshapiro.com

Your Body Speaks Your Mind: Decoding the Emotional, Psychological, and Spiritual Messages That Underlie Illness. Sounds True (2006)

INTRODUCTION

The Body Mind Appreciation Exercise leads you through each part of your body, so you can experience how much love there is within you, developing a deep appreciation and gratitude for your whole being, including those parts that are hurting. This practice should be done lying down, using a small pillow for your head and a light blanket to keep you warm. As you settle, release any constrictive clothing; remove your watch or glasses. Arms should be beside your body, palms facing upward. Feet are slightly apart, eyes are closed.

This is the body mind appreciation practice.

Make yourself comfortable.

Lying down. Eyes are closed.

This practice develops a deep awareness and gratitude for every part of your body — even those places that may be hurting. It invites you to recognize that those parts that are in pain are an integral part of your wholeness. And that healing comes through appreciation and gratitude, rather than through resistance.

Take a deep breath and let it out slowly.

Feel yourself relaxing, your body becoming heavier, as it sinks into the floor.

Focus on the flow of your breath as it enters and leaves.

Watching your body rising and falling with each breath.

Just letting go and relaxing.

We are going to work through your whole body, starting at the top.

So, begin by becoming aware of your head. This is your central control. The head maintains all your bodily functions, yet it is also your place of awareness, insight, intelligence and perception. It forms a pivotal axis between heaven and earth, containing both your highest spiritual awareness and your more earthly individual self. Thank your head for this vital role that it plays in maintaining your entire well-being.

Now, bring your attention to your face, the part of you that meets and greets the world first, that is representative of your innermost feelings. Thank your face for its beauty and sensitivity. Now come to your mouth, where you taste reality as it first comes to you. Here also, you share the depth of your being with others, through your whispering, talking, singing. You show your love with your kisses and endearments. Your jaw enables this to happen while your teeth chew over your reality and act as a gateway through which it has to pass. Thank your mouth, jaw, and teeth for the constant service they give you. Breathe into them, releasing any tension, feeling a deep gratitude for them.

Now, come to your nose, where the scent of life fills your being and you bring oxygen into your lungs. Deeply thank your nose for the sweet smells that fill your being and for the precious oxygen that gives you life.

Now, bring attention to your eyes, which are the windows to your soul, expressing your inner being. Tears are the waters of healing. Thank your tears for freely expressing your feelings. Thank your eyes for the vision that gives you so much joy, appreciating the precious gift of sight.

Now, come to your ears, where you receive your world through sound. The ears also give you balance and equilibrium. Appreciate and thank your ears for the sounds of life they bring to you and for keeping you poised and graceful in your movement.

Become aware of your neck and throat, the bridge between head and heart. Here, you swallow your reality, taking in sensations from the world around you, and here you express your heartfelt feelings. The neck enables you to be open and flexible so you can see on all sides. Breathe into your neck. Thank it deeply and feel that gratitude pouring down your throat, soothing and loving.

Now, bring your attention to your shoulders that carry your world of responsibilities while enabling you to express your feeling through your arms. Thank your shoulders for the load you carry. Breathe into them and feel the warmth of love pouring through them, releasing and relaxing.

Now, become aware of your arms. Through them you can open your heart by reaching out to embrace, hug, and share your love. And through them, you express your inner creativity. Feel the love pouring through your arms and thank them for that strength and caring.

Now, come to your hands, as here you share, express and create, touch and caress. Thank your hands for giving so consistently.

Now, feel the whole of your back as it lies on the floor, stretching from your neck to your buttocks—feel the muscles, the ribs, and the different vertebrae. Breathe into each bone, each muscle. Here are issues to do with courage, power, and assertiveness. Your spine gives you dignity and pride. Your ability to walk freely and with uprightness. Thank your back and feel a deep gratitude for the love it supports you with, each day.

Become aware of your buttocks. This is where you sit on things you want no one else to see. Relax any tension in your buttocks and thank them for supporting you and holding you with love.

Now, come to the front of your body and become aware of your chest. For a woman, here is tenderness and sensitivity, nourishment and comfort. For a man, there is strength, power, and bravery here — protection and gentleness. Thank and appreciate your chest for the love that nourishes and protects you.

Now, bring your attention to your hips. The pelvis allows you to stand upright and move forward. Thank your pelvis, which holds your whole being in a circle of strength. Within this area, lie your genitals. Extend your deep appreciation and gratitude to this tender part of you that enables you to be intimate with another and gives you such great pleasure.

Now, feel both your legs in their entirety, how they enable you to stand tall, to hold your own ground and place in the world. To walk forward, to run, to jump, to dance. Feel the warmth of love and gratitude, pouring through your legs that carry you through so many different times and through so many different places.

Now, focus on your knees. Kneeling is an act of surrendering the ego and of releasing pride. The knees allow you to move with flexibility and grace, to bend and to kneel. Deeply thank your knees for all that they do. Feel your gratitude for them.

Now, bring your attention to your feet. Feel each part of your feet. The toes. The arches. The soles. How they are your foundation and carry you through your life. How they give you direction and purpose. How they connect you to the earth. Thank your feet and feel a deep appreciation for all that they do. Recognize the love that they offer every day.

Now, we come to your inner body, starting with your digestive system. Become aware of your mouth, leading to your throat, to your stomach, where your outer and inner realities meet. And where all your emotions are assimilated. Breathe into your stomach. Feel a softness and gentleness. Feel as if it is filled with your love and gratitude.

Now, become aware of your abdomen and intestines, where you absorb nourishment from your food and release what you no longer need. Here you absorb your reality, integrating and processing all your feelings. Relax any tension in your belly. Soft belly. Soft belly. Feel a love and gratitude for your belly, for its constant absorbing and digesting so that you may be nourished. And take that awareness to your rectum, releasing any tension, feeling a deep gratitude for this process of eliminating whatever you no longer need.

Now, focus on your kidneys and your bladder. This wonderful waste disposal system is constantly cleansing you of negativity and unwanted emotions. Thank your kidneys and your bladder and appreciate the love they give you. Your liver is also a part of your digestive system, as it detoxifies and processes your reality. Breathe into your liver and thank it for working so tirelessly for you to stay healthy.

Now, bring your attention to your lungs. The gift of life is given to you in each breath you take, from your nose to your lungs and from there to every cell in your body. Breathe deeply, filling your whole being, and let it out slowly, releasing any tension. Through your breath, you nourish every cell with love. Feel that love in your lungs as you breathe in and out.

Now, become aware of your heart and the blood that circulates within you. With each breath, feel your heart opening, softening, releasing. This is your center of love, fearlessness, and compassion. Breathe into your heart with gratitude and appreciation and feel the love that is in your heart pouring through your blood, filling every cell. Thank your heart and blood for the life they give you and for the love that nourishes you.

Now, become aware of your immune system that recognizes foreign substances and stops them from doing you any harm. Your immune system cells circulate throughout your blood. In your lymph system, in your thymus gland, throughout your whole being, protecting you. This is your ability to protect yourself against illness. Feel a deep appreciation and gratitude for your immune system. Thank it for working so hard to maintain your well being.

Now, become aware of your nervous system, stretching from your brain all the way down your spine and out into every part of your body. Constantly sending and receiving information, enabling you to move and to communicate. Deeply thank your nerves. Appreciate how they give you the sensation and awareness that make your life so enjoyable.

Now, feel your bones, your joints, your muscles, your flesh. Feel your skin that covers your whole physical body, creating a protective boundary between you and the world and extend your appreciation and gratitude.

Now, bring your attention to any area that is in pain or discomfort and hold that part of you that is hurting, in love. Use your breath to release any resistance. This is a part of you, not separate from you, and it needs your love as much as every other part. Feel a deep gratitude for the pain, for it is teaching you to love more deeply. For it is there to help you grow. Know that the pain is a part of you and is just as precious as any other part.

Now, hold your whole body and thank it for its enduring service, for its love.

Let your gratitude be for your physical body, as well as for your thoughts, your feelings, and your spirit of life.

Bring your attention to the energy within you, flowing throughout you, your life force. Feel the power of this life force.

Breathe into it and become one with it.

With each in breath, feel the life force, filling you with love.

Visualize yourself as whole, as healed.

Feel your body lying on the floor and the life force as it pours through you, like a gentle wave back and forth.

Know this loving life force to be your healer.

Silently repeat,

"May I be well. May all of me be well. May the healing power of love be with me always.

May I be well. May all of me be well. May the healing power of love be with me always."

Take a deep breath and let it go. Become aware of your fingers and toes and begin to move them. Keeping your eyes closed, when you are ready, roll over on your side and gently sit up. Become aware of your presence, sitting in the room. Feel the power of love within and all around you. It is with you always.

194

INSTALLATION OF IMAGINAL RESOURCES EMPLOYING ALTERNATING TACTILE BILATERAL STIMULATION

SAFE PLACE

Ricky Greenwald cautions, ". . . many therapists will religiously teach their clients Safe Place. . . without necessarily understanding that Safe Place is only intended as one example of a class of interventions that can help clients to learn to self-soothe and build affect tolerance." (Greenwald, 2006). In her latest book, *Tapping In* (Parnell, 2008), Laurel Parnell writes, "In the early days of EMDR we discovered that bilateral stimulation could also be used in a focused way to activate and strengthen certain resources within our clients." Seems like everybody loves Safe Place. "We found that directing clients to focus on a (imaginal) safe place and then adding short sets of bilateral stimulation worked even better than imagery alone to calm them and provide them with a sense of control over their distress. This practice, called 'installing a safe place' helped traumatized people feel safer and was used by therapists prior to beginning EMDR sessions."

Resourcing has proven successful in many clients. (If a client is unable to use this resourcing method, it is not advised to use the EMDR protocol for reprocessing trauma). Clinicians can facilitate the development and installation of many different kinds of resources to help strengthen egos and stabilize clients — especially those who have histories of abuse and/or neglect in their childhood. Although resource installation has become a mainstay prior to an individual EMDR session, Parnell and others have begun using this technique as a stand-alone procedure. In contrast to EMDR for trauma processing, resourcing work is kept focused exclusively on the development of positive, healing resources followed by a short set of alternating bilateral stimulation (Korn and Leeds, 2002; Parnell, 2008).

In the resourcing process, the client is directed in a multi-sensory guided imagery exercise, that includes deliberate enhancement and awareness of his/her sensory, somatic and affective experience of the resource being installed. Clinicians should ask explicit questions, e.g., during the development of a safe/comfortable place, the clinician asks, what do you see now? What about when you look all around? Are there any sounds? Smells? What is the temperature? What makes this place so comfortable? What do you like about it? When you look around again, experiencing the sights, sounds, smells, how do you feel? Where do you feel that in your body?

When the resource is located and being vividly experienced by the client, the clinician asks the client for a word or phrase that captures his/her feeling state, e.g., relax, calm, strong and solid, the beach, chill. . . anything. Really. The clinician then directs the client to "breathe into that" while applying alternating bilateral tactile stimulation (ABTS) for a short duration, i.e. either the clinician taps on the client's hands (that are resting on the client's knees) or alternatively teaches the client to tap on his/her own knees. The tapping should last for no longer than ten seconds or two full breaths. (It is important to keep the ABTS short. In addition, the clinician should be continuously monitoring the client's affect, as positive resources can easily turn negative or become contaminated with negative associations. Even when keeping the sets short it can happen, so continuous monitoring and checking in with the client is essential.)

Theory behind resource installation: The ABTS is applied to strengthen the associations between the client's anchor word, sights, sounds, smells, tactile sensations and his/her visceral response and the feeling state. ("The general idea is an old one, that any two cells or systems of cells that are repeatedly active at the same time will tend to become 'associated', so that activity in one facilitates activity in the other . . . The theory is commonly evoked to explain some types of associative learning in which simultaneous activation of cells leads to pronounced increases in synaptic strength. Such learning is known as Hebbian learning — often summarized as "neurons that fire together, wire together." (Hebb, 1949))

THIS IS NOT A SCRIPT; IT'S A REFERENCE

Remember the client already has the resource. Clinicians are just helping to evoke it, by getting the client to pay attention to his/her sensory experience (all or most of his/her senses should be activated); his/her body sensations; and his/her emotions while experiencing the resource. The client should (cognitively) label his/her experience. The clinician then adds ABTS (ten seconds or two full breaths is fine) to strengthen those connections.

1. Have the client close his/her eyes or find a spot on which to focus.

2. Have the client pay attention to his/her breath, finding a quiet place within him/herself.

3. Invite the client to breathe deeply, attempting to make the exhalation longer than the inhalation, relaxing and releasing with each breath.

4. Have the client bring to mind the resource of Safe/Comfortable Place. Imagining it as fully as possible. Have him/her notice what (s)he is seeing, hearing, smelling, touching. Ask what sensations are felt on the skin. What does (s)he taste? What does (s)he feel in his/her body when in this place? Give the client all the time (s)he may need.

5. Ask the client to report when (s)he feels like (s)he is really there.

6. If it is positive, apply a short set of ABTS (ten seconds or two breaths is fine).

7. Instruct the client to check in again. Ask what the client is noticing? If the resource is strengthening and remains positive, continue to add ABTS (Remember, it is important that the resource feel completely positive. Clinician should be willing and encouraging even if several resources turn negative. Treat them all as tentative experiments, where there can be no failure, e.g., Okay, maybe this place wasn't altogether positive, so let's try a different one — one that is all positive).

If a distressing thought, feeling, or memory arises, have the client imagine placing it in a container. The container can be anything that can safely hold the material that has come up. In his book, *Psychotherapeutic Interventions for Emotion Regulation: EMDR and Bilateral*

Stimulation for Affect Management (Omaha, 2004), John Omaha recommends creating an imaginal container that could serve to limit the pressure and intensity of feelings in the service of preventing affective flooding or client overwhelm. The imaginal container can be used to contain distress, emotions and problems in and out of session. It can also hold material that emerges during traumatic reprocessing sessions that may not be directly related to the traumatic memory, yet interfere with the client's ability to process. The container can also be used to store yet unresolved elements of traumatic material when *closing down* incomplete sessions.

IMAGINAL CONTAINER

Instructions: Have the client bring up an image of a container — one that is big enough to hold each and every disturbing thing—but, discourage the client from focusing on any particular thing or image. Encourage the client to make the container as real as possible, noticing its heavy, secure lid. Explain to the client that (s)he may put in or take out whatever (s)he wants any time that (s)he wants. Explain to the client that this container should be labeled with something to the effect that it should be only when it would be in the service his/her healing. Instruct the client that at no time should any part of him/herself be placed in the container. (For ego states work and Internal Family Systems work, the reader is referred to Forgash and Copely, 2007 and Schwartz, 1995). The client should imagine placing all the distressing or disturbing material into the container and sealing it tightly. As the name suggests, when containers are installed, the client should feel as though (s)he has the ability to contain his/her own affect. It should also produce feelings of agency and control over the traumatic material. (*See You're Grounded!* — *Protective Container Exercise*, page 129)

NURTURING FIGURES

Nurturing figures can be anyone — real or imaginary figures from the present or the past, imaginary inner guides, or animals. Instruct clients to look for those people who were loving, safe, nurturing figures. Perhaps people from his/her past or current life that are, or have been important sources of comfort and care. Alternatively, these figures can be from movies, TV, books, or historical figures. Could be anybody, really. Anybody by whom the client feels — or could feel — nurtured. Could be Glinda, the good witch, a guardian angel, fairy godmother, Mary, Jesus, a Native American elder, Buddha, goddesses like Kwan Yin or Tara, or Mother Teresa. Anybody, really. Clients with a dearth of nurturing figures abound in our offices. The method that has served me best has been not to ask for a figure, but to ask the question, Has there ever been a time when you felt taken care of? (S)he may have to dig, but clients can usually come up with an incident. Then we deliberately enhance the nurturing quality of it — sights, sounds, body sensations, and emotions, then add the alternating bilateral stimulation to strengthen the connections. (The caveat remains: lots of resources turn negative quickly because they serve as reminders of deprivation which tends to contaminate the new figures, so keep it tentative and let go as often as necessary.)

Animals can also serve as nurturing figures — childhood or present-day pets, a power animal or mythological creature. Any animal, really. The clinician may suggest that the client use his/her adult self as a nurturer. That aspect of the client may be contacted by having him/her recall times when (s)he cared for another. Perhaps (s)he remembers holding a child or petting an animal. When developing the nurturing figure resource, it is important to imagine the figure in its nurturing aspect. This can include memories or images of the figure being nurturing. For example, you might think of a time when your Mom held you in her arms and sang to you. This image represents the quality of nurture to be strengthened and made available for later use. Your Mom may also serve as a protective figure, but in that case the conjured image would be of her acting in a protective vs. nurturing way. The client should feel the quality of nurture from the figure.

Protector Figures

Protector figures can be anyone. Could be a real person — someone from childhood or present life. It is important that when you think of your protectors that you believe that they would defend you against harm. Someone who has had — or will have your back if you were to be threatened. Memories of positive experiences with real-life protector figures can be used. Like nurturing figures, protector figures can include anybody. Really. Parents, grandparents, friends, partners, cats, and rats and elephants, action heroes, superheroes, or mythic figures. The clinician may even suggest that the client use his/her own protective adult self. Again when developing the protective figure, it is important to imagine the figure in its protective aspect, i.e., when they are keeping you or someone else from harm. The client should feel the quality of protection from the figure.

Cited and Recommended Readings for Resource Development and Installation

- *Healing the Heart of Trauma and Dissociation with EMDR and Ego State Therapy* by Carol Forgash (Editor), Margaret Copeley (Editor) Springer Publishing Company; (2007) ISBN-10: 0826146961 SBN-13: 978-0826146960

- *Internal Family Systems Therapy* by Richard Schwartz, The Guilford Press; (1997) ISBN-10: 1572302720 ISBN-13: 978-1572302723

- *Psychotherapeutic Interventions for Emotion Regulation: EMDR and Bilateral Stimulation for Affect Management* by John Omaha, W. W. Norton & Company; 1st edition (2004) ISBN-10: 0393703959 ISBN-13: 978-0393703955

- *EMDR: Within a Phase Model of Trauma-Informed Treatment (Maltreatment, Trauman, and Interpersonal Aggression)* by Ricky Greenwald, Publisher: Haworth Press (2007) ISBN-10: 0789032163 ISBN-13: 978-0789032164

- *A Therapist's Guide to EMDR: Tools and Techniques for Successful Treatment* by Laurel Parnell, W. W. Norton; (2006) ISBN-10: 0393704815 ISBN-13: 978-0393704815

- *Tapping In: A Step-by-Step Guide to Activating Your Healing Resources Through Bilateral Stimulation* by Laurel Parnell, Publisher: Sounds True, Incorporated (January 1, 2008) ISBN-10: 1591797888 ISBN-13: 978-1591

- Preliminary Evidence of Efficacy for EMDR Resource Development and Installation in the Stabilization Phase of Treatment of Complex Post-traumatic Stress Disorder. Deborah L. Korn, Psy.D., Private practice, Andrew M. Leeds, Ph.D., Private practice, *Journal of Clinical Psychology* (2002). For full article: 2http://www.emdr.nl/acrobat/Emdrml.pdf

Working Through Trauma: Eye Movement Desensitization and Reprocessing (EMDR)

About thirty years ago, Francine Shapiro (1989) modified Wolpe's (1958) systematic desensitization therapy by replacing progressive muscle relaxation with purposefully induced eye movements. Designed originally as a treatment for traumatic memories, Shapiro dubbed it, Eye Movement Desensitization (EMD). The general idea of it was; the client identified a traumatic target memory, then the therapist would have the client verbalize a self-referent (global, irrational) negative cognition associated with the memory (e.g., I am bad or It's my fault) along with a positive cognition (e.g., I am fine or I did the best I could) to replace the negative one. The therapist would then wave his/her fingers back and forth in front of the client's eyes, instructing the client to track her fingers visually while focusing on the target memory. After each set of 10-12 eye movements, the therapist would ask the client to provide ratings of distress (Subjective Units of Distress or SUDS) and strength of belief in the positive cognition (Validity of Cognition or VoC). The therapist would repeat this procedure until the client's distress subsided and belief in the positive cognition increased.

It is a pretty simple protocol — easy to master. Indeed, the protocol is easy to master, however, when administered by clinicians lacking requisite knowledge of trauma's sequelae, this simple protocol proves challenging, fear-inducing, and oftentimes traumatizing for clinicians and re-traumatizing for clients. So there's no misinterpretation of the last sentence, *the EMDR protocol is not dangerous.* However, any type of trauma work that deliberately activates traumatic memory networks without insisting that the client and the clinician are adequately prepared to tolerate the effects of that activation is dangerous and irresponsible.

Throughout trauma treatment, the clinician must continuously and vigilantly attend and re-attend to client safety and stabilization. Regardless of the type of trauma processing employed, there can be no substitute for the following: the therapeutic relationship; clinical assessment and judgment; an explicit crisis plan; and instruction in — and acquisition of — skills for affect and emotion regulation, arousal reduction, and distress tolerance prior to trauma work.

> . . . EMDR is a trauma resolution method. A trauma resolution method is most appropriately offered as a late-stage intervention within a comprehensive trauma-informed treatment approach. As therapists who use EMDR, we don't just say to a new client, "Hi, I'm Dr. X. Tell me the worst thing that ever happened to you and follow my fingers." The treatment

approach must include a case conceptualization that specifies how the trauma memories are contributing to the present complaint — otherwise why do EMDR? And the treatment approach must also provide a systematic way of helping the client to get to a point of being willing and able to tolerate, and benefit from, EMDR. (Greenwald, 2006)*

How do I know if my client is ready for trauma reprocessing? (Parnell, 2007)

1. Do you have rapport, i.e., a trusting relationship with an empathic bond?
2. Is the client committed to safety and treatment?
3. Can clients handle high levels of affect? Is the client able to benefit from installation of resources including guided visualization for safety, protection, and nurture?
4. What other supports can the client consistently count on outside of therapy?
5. Does the client require a medical consult? Does the client require a psychiatric and/or medication evaluation?
6. Is the client in active addiction? Does the client self injure or engage in other self-harming behaviors? (Degree of severity)
7. Is the client currently mentally unstable or currently decompensating?
8. Does the client have a DID diagnosis? Is the client's preferred method coping dissociation? (Dissociative Experience Scale II see assessment section for copies)
9. Is the client involved in an active legal case?

Four Essential Elements for EMDR Protocol (Parnell, 2007)

1. Create safety
2. Stimulate traumatic neural network
3. Add alternating bilateral stimulation
4. End with safety

---

* Excerpted from: *The Peanut Butter and Jelly Problem: In Search of a Better EMDR Training Model,* Ricky Greenwald, Child Trauma Institute, Greenfield, MA, USA, May 2006

The Four Essential Elements for EMDR Protocol

(Parnell, 2007)

1. Create safety
2. Stimulate traumatic neural network
3. Add alternating bilateral stimulation
4. End with safety

The Original 8 Phase EMDR Protocol

(Shapiro, 1995, 2001, 2002, 2005)

Phase 1: Client History and Treatment Planning:

A complete biopsychosocial history, including medical status, family and childhood history — including neglect, abuse, and traumatic events (big "T", i.e., events that everyone would consider traumatic and little "t" trauma, i.e., idiosyncratic events perceived as traumatic) and any/all current symptoms. With this information, the clinician and client proceed to co-create a plan for treatment.

Phase 2: Preparation

Clinician prepares the client for trauma work:

1. Safety, rapport, and trust must be established between the client and clinician.
2. The EMDR process should be explained fully; client should have a basic understanding of EMDR; effects and side effects and an expectation of what will happen in and after sessions.
3. All concerns and fears are addressed; safety procedures are discussed and put in place.
4. The therapist resources the client with self-soothing, affect regulation, and arousal reduction techniques.
5. If applicable, the client chooses the type of bilateral stimulation — auditory, tactile, or eye movement.

Phase 3: Assessment

The assessment phase begins the core of the EMDR process. The client chooses the traumatic material, i.e., the target memory for the session. (S)he is asked to evoke the image that represents the worst part of the traumatic memory. Linking words to the image (or experience) that express his/her current global, irrational, negative cognition. The client is then asked for a positive cognition, i.e. what (s)he would like to believe about him/herself in place of current negative cognition. Using a seven-point VOC scale, (0=false – 7=completely true) the client assesses the validity of the new positive cognition relative to the target experience. The client describes the emotions associated with the target memory and rates the disturbance on a (0-10) scale — Subjective Units of Disturbance/Distress Scale (SUDS). Finally, the client describes the related body sensations.

Phase 4: Desensitization

The desensitization process begins with the client holding in focus the image that represents the worst of the incident; his/her negative cognitions; emotions and body sensations associated with the traumatic incident. A set (or round) of Alternating Bilateral Stimulation is introduced. This may take the form of hand movements or moving lights in the client's field of vision; alternating auditory tones; or alternating taps on knees or hands.

These sets of Alternating Bilateral Stimulation may last from thirty seconds to several minutes, depending on the client's response. At the completion of each set, the client is asked to clear his/her mind and to allow whatever comes into awareness. After giving a short description of what has come up, another set (or round) of Alternating Bilateral Stimulation is introduced. Over many sets of bilateral stimulation, the therapist guides the client through the processing of all the incident's associated material.

Phase 5: Installation of Positive Cognition

When the processing of the traumatic material is complete, as measured by the amount of residual disturbance of the incident (SUDS=0), the positive cognition is then revisited and re-scaled (0–7 on the VoC scale) as to its validity in the presence of the original incident. Sets (or rounds) of Alternating Bilateral Stimulation are again applied until the positive cognition is experienced as being totally valid (VoC=7).

Phase 6: Body Scan

Once the desensitization phase is complete, the client is asked to once again evoke the original incident and mentally scan his/her body. If sensations or lack of sensations are reported, short sets (or rounds) of Alternating Bilateral Stimulation are then applied until the sensation subsides or a positive feeling is experienced.

Phase 7: Closure

It is very common for clients to continue processing traumatic material for days or even weeks after a session. The client should be informed and prepared to deal with any vivid dreams, strong feelings, intrusive thoughts, or recollections of past experiences. Clients should be instructed to write them down and bring them back to session. If the client becomes overwhelmed or flooded, he/she should be instructed to call the therapist and the therapist should be prepared to return calls in a timely manner.

Phase 8: Re-evaluation

At the beginning of the next session, the client assesses and reviews the week, talking about any new sensations or experiences. The disturbance of the previous session's target experience is once again assessed and SUDS level re-rated. If residual disturbance or distress remains, then it should be targeted; if none present, then the client and clinician decide on the next target.

The eight-stage protocol is a tribute to its developer's clinical, as well as research acumen and ability. Dr. Shapiro developed a protocol that was simultaneously the therapeutic intervention and its measure for outcomes. The Likert scales, while essential in research and academia, are at times an impediment to clinical practice, i.e., although necessary to empirically prove this method's efficacy, the request that clients quantify their levels of distress, *while distressed*, is virtually impossible.

Laurell Parnell recognized the need for a "kinder, gentler protocol" — one that neither insists on numeric measurements nor requires clients to oscillate between traumatic activation and deactivation for the sake of the accuracy of the measurements. When a client is visibly activated, (s)he is without access to the left hemisphere where logic and language reside, Therefore pressing for measurements is, if not inhumane, at least extremely frustrating for the client.

What follows is Parnell's modified protocol. It seems preferable given that our clients are able to report an increase or decrease in distress levels without using the scales.

Modified EMDR Session Protocol (Parnell, 2007)

1. Identify the problem.
2. Resource client-using guided visualization, evoke and install safe place and/or protection and support; and/or nurturing figure.
3. Identify an image or picture that represents the worst part of the memory.
4. Identify emotions.
5. Identify body sensations.
6. Identify NC.
7. SUDS: SKIP.
8. Desensitize (Near the end of the processing, i.e., when the negative affect has significantly subsided, then you can get a SUDS level and positive cognition).
9. Get a SUDS.
10. Get the PC.
11. Install the PC. Skip the VoC.
12. Perform a body scan. (Skip if time limited.)
13. Closure: Be sure that client is properly debriefed; currently embodied; and oriented to time, place, and person.

Cited and Recommended Readings for EMDR Reprocessing Traumatic Material

1. Brown, Scheflin & Hammond (1998). *Memory, Trauma Treatment, and the Law.*

2. Greenwald (2002). *Trauma and Juvenile Delinquency: Theory, Research, and Interventions.*

   - (1999). *Eye Movement Desensitization Reprocessing (EMDR) in Child and Adolescent Therapy.*

3. Herman, Judith. *Trauma and Recovery.* New York: Basic Books, Harper Collins Publishers.

4. Levine, Peter. (1997). *Waking the Tiger.* Berkeley, CA: North Atlantic Books.

   - *Healing Trauma. Restoring the Wisdom of Your Body.* Boulder Colorado: Sounds True.

   - *Sexual Healing. Transforming the Sacred Wound.* Boulder, Colorado: Sounds True.

5. Lipke (1999). *Emdr And Psychotherapy Integration: Theoretical and Clinical Suggestions With Focus On Traumatic Stress.*

6. Manfield (Ed.) (2003). *EMDR Casebook*: Expanded second edition.

7. Parnell (2007). *A Therapist's Guide to EMDR.*

   - (1999). *EMDR in the Treatment of Adults Abused as Children.*

   - (1997) *Transforming Trauma: EMDR.*

8. Naparstek, B. (2005). *Invisible Heroes: Survivors of Trauma and How They Heal.* New York: Bantam Books

9. Rothchild, Babette. (2000). *The Body Remembers. The Psychophysiology of Trauma and Trauma Treatment.* New York: W.W.Norton & Company.

10. Shapiro, F. (2001). *Eye Movement Desensitization and Reprocessing*, Second Edition. Second edition of the original (1995) EMDR text.

Working Through Trauma: Somatic Experiencing

According to Peter Levine, trauma is healed through the process of discharging excess survival energy. We do this by:

1. Uncoupling fear from the immobility response.

2. Moving out of immobility.

3. Completing the arousal cycle.

Renegotiation of Trauma vs. Reliving Trauma

According to Levine, it is not necessary to relive a trauma in order to process it. In Somatic Experiencing, we "renegotiate" our old traumas. Renegotiation employs elements of the original trauma combined with strengths and resources that were unavailable at the time of the event. (Most clients with a history of childhood sexual abuse were without physical and psychological resources at the time of trauma, therefore, when traumatic memories are activated, the client, literally, has exactly those same resources, or lack thereof, that he/she had at the time of original incident. This is why resourcing the client thoroughly is essential before we begin trauma work with clients: i.e. establishment of trust and rapport with the therapist; installation of safe place and inner advisor; grounding and muscle tensing exercises; skin as a barrier exercise; adult self/child self relationship development; and adequate external support). Interweaving these missing pieces with the incomplete defensive actions of the trauma creates a new and complete experience. Completion transforms the trauma, strengthening us and building greater resistance to future traumas.

Research has demonstrated that physical sensations and action patterns are the very foundation of consciousness, by learning to "Focus" — paying close attention to our internal experience — clients find healing ways of working with what Eugene Gendlin calls the "felt sense." According to Gendlin, "Focusing is direct access to a bodily knowing." Eugene Gendlin's use of the word refers to the way in which something at first blurry and unclear gradually becomes clearer, as if one is focusing a camera. Focusing was first identified in the 1950s by Gendlin, a philosopher and psychotherapist, during his research with Carl Rogers into what made psychotherapy effective. The conclusion he came to was that those who benefited most from therapy had the ability to sense vague, still unformed feelings in their body and connect this sensing (which he names the 'felt sense') with words and images that described it. This meant being able to discover what was not yet fully known, which in itself could allow the process to move forward. He noticed that during the process there would often be an opening or release in the body, perhaps accompanied by a sigh, and this he described as a 'felt shift.'

Gendlin recognized that those clients who could relate to their experience in this way already had access to a particular skill. What he came to call Focusing was developed as a means of teaching this skill to people who did not access it so easily. He initially formulated the Focusing process as a series of six steps: clearing a space, locating a felt sense, finding a 'handle' (a way of describing the felt sense), resonating the handle with the felt sense to see whether it fits, asking "What makes this issue/feeling so . . . ?" and finally receiving the shift if it comes.

For more information the reader is referred to:
The Focusing Institute website: http://www.focusing.org

Every Somatic Experiencing session has certain basic elements. These may appear in different sequences, depending on individual needs and conditions — but overall, the following will give you a sense of what a session looks like.

1. **Tracking.** In renegotiation, client becomes mindful of body sensations, images, behaviors, emotions, and thoughts. Tracking encourages a heightened state of body awareness, allowing client to become conscious of previously hidden instinctual responses.

2. **Activation.** The nervous system, muscles, body, and mind are tensed in preparation for defensive action. The brain releases chemicals to provide the necessary energy.

3. **Defeat/Overwhelm.** Feelings of complete helplessness, defeat, and being overwhelmed constitute the psychological experience of the immobility response. These feelings may arise again as part of re-experiencing some aspects of the original event — however, the client will not actually relive the trauma. This would not be helpful; in fact, experiencing defeat/overwhelm again and again can actually be harmful.

4. **Resourcing.** Client's instinctive resources for successful self-defense, overwhelmed in the original event, become available through the tracking process. During the resourcing phase of renegotiation, the therapist (support is critical here) guides the client to reclaim these tools.

5. **Pendulating.** As the client becomes resourced, he/she will find a natural rhythm that guides him/her back and forth between the past (unresourced) defeat and the present (resourced) experience, allowing for the formation of a new experience.

6. **Grounding and Centering.** Trauma disconnects people from their bodies. Grounding and centering reconnects the client directly with resources naturally available in his/her own body.

7. **Strength and Resilience.** Grounding and centering also reconnect the client to a sense of strength and resiliency. With this awareness, client is poised for successful defensive action.

8. **Natural Aggression.** When the client is free to recognize and allow instinctive responses, the client will know when fighting is an appropriate response to a threat — and can discharge the activated energy by following through.

9. **Running.** Likewise, client will know instinctively when the right response is to run, and can discharge energy, as appropriate, by doing so.

10. **Uncoupling.** Undischarged energy intensifies fear and couples it with immobility. Discharging this energy uncouples fear from immobility, allowing the client to move beyond trauma and toward transformation.

11. **Orientation.** After the client emerges from immobility, the therapist will reorient him/her to a world that often appears quite different from before.

12. **Completion.** Completing the cycle discharges the energy that had been fueling the symptoms of trauma. Now the client's symptoms are free to diminish in strength and frequency, or even to disappear altogether.

According to Levine, body sensations, rather than intense emotion, hold the key to healing trauma. He advises conscious awareness of emotional reactions within, but keeping the focus of attention on the manner in which the body is experiencing these emotions in the form of sensations and thoughts.

Various Types of Trauma-Focused Therapies

Following is list of some of them with short descriptions and how to locate further information for each:

ACCELERATED EXPERIENTIAL DYNAMIC PSYCHOTHERAPY

Developed by: Diana Fosha, Ph.D.

Summary:

AEDP (Accelerated Experiential-Dynamic Psychotherapy) is a transformation-based, healing-oriented model of psychotherapy developed by Dr. Diana Fosha. Our aim is to foster the emergence of new and healing emotional experiences for and with our patients. Intense emotional experience and suffering are part and parcel of being alive; they are also—if properly regulated—the pathways to resources and resilience. But when these experiences, bad or good, threaten to overwhelm us, we need others to help us regulate them. Being alone with unbearable emotions is at the root of psychopathology. When relationships fail to help regulate what is too much to bear alone, people resort to defensive strategies. Long-term reliance on these defenses disrupts growth and development, blocks access to adaptive resources, and contributes to the pain and difficulties that lead people to seek treatment. In Accelerated Experiential-Dynamic Psychotherapy, our goal is to be together with our patients as they process intense emotional experiences which were previously feared, be they painful or joyful. Furthermore, we are not just bundles of pathology: Lodged deeply in our brains and bodies lie innate, wired-in dispositions for healing and self-righting. Accelerated Experiential-Dynamic Psychotherapy also aims to activate these naturally occurring, adaptive change processes. When the self has reason to hope that a relationship has such potential, defenses can be put aside and individuals can risk leading with their genuine, spontaneous responses. It is what Accelerated Experiential-Dynamic Psychotherapy seeks to facilitate through its affirming, emotionally engaged therapeutic stance and its relational, experiential, and integrative techniques

Excerpt from Accelerated Experiential Dynamic Psychotherapy

Website: http://www.aedpinstitute.com

ACCEPTANCE AND COMMITMENT THERAPY

Developed by: Steven C. Hayes, Ph.D., Kirk D. Strosahl, Ph.D., Spencer Smith, Ph.D., Kelly G. Wilson, Ph.D.

Summary:

Developed within a coherent theoretical and philosophical framework, Acceptance and Commitment Therapy is a unique empirically based psychological intervention that uses acceptance and mindfulness strategies, together with commitment and behavior change strategies, to increase psychological flexibility. Psychological flexibility means contacting the present moment fully as a conscious human being, and based on what the situation affords, changing or persisting in behavior in the service of chosen values. Based on Relational Frame Theory, Acceptance and Commitment Therapy illuminates the ways that language entangles clients into futile attempts to wage war against their own inner lives. Through metaphor, paradox, and experiential exercises clients learn how to make healthy contact with thoughts, feelings, memories, and physical sensations that have been feared and avoided. Clients gain the skills to recontextualize and accept these private events, develop greater clarity about personal values, and commit to needed behavior change"

Excerpt from Acceptance & Commitment Therapy.

Website: http://www.contextualpsychology.org/act.

DIALECTICAL BEHAVIOR THERAPY

Developed by: Marsha M. Linehan

Summary:

In the late 1970s, Marsha M. Linehan attempted to apply standard Cognitive Behavior Therapy (CBT) to the problems of adult women with histories of chronic suicide attempts, suicidal ideation, urges to self-harm, and self-mutilation. Trained as a behaviorist, she was interested in treating discrete behaviors; however, through consultation with colleagues, she concluded that she was treating women who met criteria for Borderline Personality (BPD).

DBT maintains that some people, due to invalidating environments during upbringing and due to biological factors as yet unknown, react abnormally to emotional stimulation. Their level of arousal goes up much more quickly, peaks at a higher level, and takes more time to return to baseline. This explains why people with Borderline Personality are known for crisis-strewn lives and extreme emotional lability (emotions that shift rapidly). Because of their past invalidation, people with Borderline Personality don't have any methods for coping with these sudden, intense surges of emotion. DBT is a method for teaching skills that will help in this task.

Briefly, Linehan hypothesizes that any comprehensive psychotherapy must meet five critical functions. The therapy must: a) enhance and maintain the client's motivation to change; b) enhance the client's capabilities; c) ensure that the client's new capabilities are generalized to all relevant environments; d) enhance the therapist's motivation to treat clients while also enhancing the therapist's capabilities; and, e) structure the environment so that treatment can take place.

Skills are acquired, strengthened, and generalized through the combination of skills groups, phone coaching (clients are instructed to call therapists for coaching prior to engaging in self harm), in vivo coaching, and homework assignments.

DBT also organizes treatment into stages and targets and, with very few exceptions, adheres strictly to the order in which problems are addressed. The organization of the treatment into stages and targets prevents DBT being a treatment that, week after week, addresses the crisis of the moment. Further, it has a logical progression that first addresses behaviors that could lead to the client's death, then behaviors that could lead to premature termination of therapy, to behaviors that destroy the quality of life, to the need for alternative skills. In other words, the first goal is to insure the client stays alive, so that the second goal (staying in therapy), results in meeting the third goal (building a better quality of life), partly through the acquisition of new behaviors (skills).

Excerpt from Behavioral Tech

Website: http://www.behavioraltech.com

THE DEVELOPMENTAL NEEDS MEETING STRATEGY (DNMS)

Developed by: Shirley Jean Schmidt, MA, LPC

Summary:

The Developmental Needs Meeting Strategy (DNMS) is an ego state therapy designed to treat a wide range of clients, symptoms, and issues. This includes adults with complex trauma wounds, such as those inflicted by physical, sexual, and verbal abuse; and with attachment wounds, such as those inflicted by parental rejection, neglect, and enmeshment. The DNMS is based on the assumption that the degree to which developmental needs were not adequately met is the degree to which a client is stuck in childhood. It starts by guiding clients to establish three internal Resources: a Nurturing Adult Self, a Protective Adult Self, and a Spiritual Core Self. Together these Resources gently help wounded child ego states get unstuck from the past by meeting their unmet developmental needs, helping them process through painful emotions, and by establishing an emotional bond. Alternating bilateral stimulation (made popular by EMDR therapy) is applied at key points in the process. The DNMS focuses special attention on healing maladaptive introjects (ego states that mimic abusive, neglectful, or dysfunctional caregivers). Since these wounded ego states cause the most trouble for clients, their healing results in a significant benefit. As introjects heal, clients report unwanted behaviors, beliefs, and emotions diminish.

Website: http://www.dnmsinstitute.com/

EMOTIONAL FREEDOM TECHNIQUE

Developed by: Gary Craig

Summary:

Emotional Freedom Technique (EFT) is a new discovery that has provided thousands with relief from pain, diseases and emotional issues. Simply stated, it is a unique version of acupuncture except you don't use needles. Instead, you stimulate well established energy meridian points on your body by tapping on them with your fingertips. The process is easy to memorize and is portable so you can do it anywhere. It launches off the Emotional Freedom Technique Discovery Statement that says . . . "The cause of all negative emotions is a disruption in the body's energy system."

Excerpt from Emotional Freedom Technique

Website: http://www.emofree.com/

EMDR

Developed by: Francine Shapiro, PhD

Summary:

Eye Movement Desensitization and Reprocessing (EMDR) integrates elements of many effective psychotherapies in structured protocols that are designed to maximize treatment effects. These include psychodynamic, cognitive behavioral, interpersonal, experiential, and body-centered therapies. EMDR is an information processing therapy and uses an eight-phase approach to address the experiential contributors of a wide range of pathologies. It attends to the past experiences that have set the groundwork for pathology, the current situations that trigger dysfunctional emotions, beliefs, and sensations, and the positive experience needed to enhance future adaptive behaviors and mental health.

During treatment, various procedures and protocols are used to address the entire clinical picture. One of the procedural elements is "dual stimulation" using either bilateral eye movements, tones, or taps. During the reprocessing phases the client attends momentarily to past memories, present triggers, or anticipated future experiences while simultaneously focusing on a set of external stimulus. During that time, clients generally experience the emergence of insight, changes in memories, or new associations. The clinician assists the client to focus on appropriate material before initiation of each subsequent set.

Excerpt from Eye Movement Desensitization and Reprocessing

EMDR Website: http://www.emdr.com/index.htm

ENERGY PSYCHOLOGY

Developed by: David Feinstein, Ph.D., Donna Eden, Fred P. Gallo, Ph.D.

Summary:

Building upon conventional therapeutic methods, Energy Psychology utilizes techniques from acupressure, yoga, qi gong, and energy medicine that teach people simple steps for initiating changes in their inner lives. It works by stimulating energy points on the surface of the skin which, when paired with specific psychological procedures, can shift the brain's electrochemistry to: Help Overcome Fear, Guilt, Shame, Jealousy, or Anger; Change Unwanted Habits and Behaviors; and Enhance the Ability to Love, Succeed, and Enjoy Life. While this is still a controversial area within the mental health field (the techniques look very strange and the claims of a growing number of practitioners seem too good to be true), evidence is mounting that these techniques are significant, powerful tools for both self-help and clinical treatment.

Excerpt from Energy Pscyhology

Website: http://innersource.net/energy_medicine/energy_medicine_main.htm

FOCUSING

Developed by: Eugene Gendlin, Ann Weiser Cornell, Barbara McGavin, Ed Campbell, Peter McMahon, Elfie Hinterkopf, Neil Friedman

Summary:

Focusing is a mode of inward bodily attention that most people don't know about yet. It is more than being in touch with your feelings and different from bodywork. Focusing occurs exactly at the interface of body-mind. It consists of specific steps for getting a body sense of how you are in a particular life situation. The body sense is unclear and vague at first, but if you pay attention it will open up into words or images and you experience a felt shift in your body. In the process of Focusing, one experiences a physical change in the way that the issue is being lived in the body. We learn to live in a deeper place than just thoughts or feelings. The whole issue looks different and new solutions arise. What are the benefits of focusing? Focusing helps to change where our lives are stuck. The felt shift that occurs during Focusing is good for the body, and is correlated with better immune functioning. More than 100 research studies have shown that Focusing is teachable and effective in many settings. Focusing decreases depression and anxiety and improves the relation to the body.

The Focusing Institute

Website: http://www.focusing.org

GESTALT THERAPY

Developed by: Fritz Perls, Laura Perls, Paul Goodman

Summary: Gestalt therapy focuses on here-and-now experience and personal responsibility. The objective, in addition to overcoming symptoms, is to become more alive, creative, and free from the blocks of unfinished issues that may diminish optimum satisfaction, fulfillment, and growth.

The theory of Gestalt therapy takes as its centerpiece two ideas. The first is that the proper focus of psychology is the experiential present moment. In contrast to approaches which look at the unknown and even unknowable, our perspective is the here and now of living. The second idea is that we are inextricably caught in a web of relationship with all things. It is only possible to truly know ourselves as we exist in relation to other things. These twin lenses, here-and-now awareness and the interactive field, define the subject matter of Gestalt therapy. Its theory provides a system of concepts describing the structure and organization of living in terms of aware relations. Its methodology, techniques, and applications . . . link this outlook to the practice of Gestalt therapy. The result is a psychology and method with a rich and unique view of everyday life, the depths and difficulties which life encompasses, and "the high side of normal," the ennobling and most creative heights of which we are capable. Gestalt therapists believe their approach is uniquely capable of responding to the difficulties and challenges of living, both in its ability to relieve us of some measure of our misery and by showing the way to some of the best we can achieve.

Excerpt from: Assoc. for the Advancement of Gestalt Therapy

Website: http://www.gestalttheory.net

HAKOMI

Developed by: Ron Kurtz

Summary:

Hakomi therapy is a form of depth psychology combining Western psychology and systems theory with Eastern philosophy and body-centered techniques. Hakomis five principles include: mindfulness, nonviolence, organicity, unity, and body-mind holism. 'Hakomi' is a Hopi word, meaning 'Who are you? — You are, who you are!' or 'How do you relate?' Hakomi has evolved into a complex, elegant, and highly effective form of psychotherapy appropriate in most therapeutic situations, including work with individuals, couples, families, groups, movement, and bodywork. It is suitable for crisis work and psychological maintenance, but it finds its full potential in the processes of growth, both personal and transpersonal, when we are committed to moving beyond our limits.

Excerpt from International Hakomi Institute

Website: http://www.hakomiinstitute.com

HYPNOSIS & HYPNOTHERAPY

Developed by: Franz Anton Mesmer, Braid, Charcot, Liebault, Bernheim, Clark Hull, Milton Erickson, J.P Sutcliffe, T.X. Barber, M.T. Orne, E.R. Hilgard, R.E. Shor, and T.R. Sarbin.

Summary:

Hypnosis is a state of inner absorption, concentration, and focused attention. It is like using a magnifying glass to focus the rays of the sun and make them more powerful. Similarly, when our minds are concentrated and focused, we are able to use our minds more powerfully. Because hypnosis allows people to use more of their potential, learning self-hypnosis is the ultimate act of self-control. While there is general agreement that certain effects of hypnosis exist, there are differences of opinion within the research and clinical communities about how hypnosis works. Recent research supports the view that hypnotic communication and suggestions effectively change aspects of the person's physiological and neurological functions. Practitioners use clinical hypnosis in three main ways. First, they encourage the use of imagination. Mental imagery is very powerful, especially in a focused state of attention. The mind seems capable of using imagery, even if it is only symbolic, to assist us in bringing about the things we are imagining. A second basic hypnotic method is to present ideas or suggestions to the patient. In a state of concentrated attention, ideas and suggestions that are compatible with what the patient wants seem to have a more powerful impact on the mind. Finally, hypnosis may be used for unconscious exploration, to better understand underlying motivations or identify whether past events or experiences are associated with causing a problem. Hypnosis avoids the critical censor of the conscious mind, which often defeats what we know to be in our best interests. The effectiveness of hypnosis appears to lie in the way in which it bypasses the critical observation and interference of the conscious mind, allowing the client's intentions for change to take effect.

Excerpt from American Society of Clinical Hypnosis

Website: http://www.asch.net

INTERNAL FAMILY SYSTEMS THERAPY

Developed by: Richard C. Schwartz, Ph.D.

Summary:

Internal Family Systems Therapy is a comprehensive approach to healing trauma and other related symptoms that includes guidelines for working with individuals, couples and families. The Internal Family Systems Therapy Model represents a new synthesis of two already existing paradigms: systems thinking and the multiplicity of the mind. It brings concepts and methods from the structural, strategic, narrative, and Bowenian schools of family therapy to the world of subpersonalities. Internal Family Systems Therapy provides practical methods to recognize and access the "higher" or "deeper" Self, so that the process of growth happens according to an "inner wisdom." In accessing the Self and healing parts, a person is not pushed, rushed, or imposed upon. The process is allowed to unfold at its own speed, and according to its own pattern.

Excerpt from The Center for Self Leadership

Website for Internal Family Systems Therapy: www.selfleadership.org

INTERPERSONAL NEUROBIOLOGY

Developed by: Dan Siegel, Allan Schore

Summary:

Interpersonal Neurobiology, a term coined by Dr. Dan Siegel, studies the way the brain grows and is influenced by personal relationships. Recent studies have discovered that brain growth occurs throughout the lifespan. IPNB explores the potential for healing trauma by using positive and secure influences on the brain. Conditions once thought to be permanent, now have the bright potential for healing and growth. IPNB has broad applications that are useful for parenting, mental health, addictions, education, health care, business professionals, and more.

Excerpt from Vanguard in Action

Website for Related Interpersonal Neurobiology: http://drdansiegel.com/

MINDFULNESS BASED COGNITIVE THERAPY

Developed by: Jon Kabat-Zinn, Zindel V. Segal, J. Mark G. Williams, John D. Teasdale, Bruno Cayoun

Summary:

Mindfulness Based Cognitive Therapy is based on the Mindfulness-based Stress Reduction (MBSR) eight week program, developed by Jon Kabat-Zinn in 1979 at the University of Massachusetts Medical Center. Research shows that MBSR is enormously empowering for patients with chronic pain, hypertension, heart disease, cancer, and gastrointestinal disorders, as well as for psychological problems such as anxiety and panic. Mindfulness-based Cognitive Therapy grew from this work. Zindel Segal, Mark Williams, and John Teasdale adapted the MBSR program so it could be used especially for people who had suffered repeated bouts of depression in their lives.

Excerpt from Mindfulness-based Cognitive Therapy

By practising in the (8 week) Mindfulness Based Cognitive Therapy classes, and by listening to CDs at home during the week, participants learn the practice of mindfulness meditation. Practices such as the Body Scan, Breathing meditation, and simple yoga allow participants to become in touch with moment-to-moment changes in the mind and the body and foster a new, 'decentered' perspective to their thoughts and feelings. MBCT also includes basic education about depression, and several exercises from cognitive therapy that show the links between thinking and feeling and how best participants can look after themselves when depression threatens to overwhelm them.

Excerpt from Oxford Cognitive Therapy Centre

Website: http://www.umassmed.edu/cfm/index.aspx

Narrative Therapy

Developed by: Michael White, David Epston

Summary:

Narrative therapy is a respectful and collaborative approach to counselling and community work. It focuses on the stories of people's lives and is based on the idea that problems are manufactured in social, cultural, and political contexts. Each person produces the meaning of their life from the stories that are available in these contexts.

Excerpt from Narrative Therapy Centre of Toronto

Narrative therapy is an approach to counselling and community work. It centres people as the experts in their own lives and views problems as separate from people. Narrative therapy assumes that people have many skills, competencies, beliefs, values, commitments, and abilities that will assist them to reduce the influence of problems in their lives.

Excerpt from The Dulwich Centre

The central idea of Narrative Therapy is: The person never is the problem. The person has a problem. A problem is something you have, not something you are. You don't have to change your nature. You have to fight the influence of the problem on your life.

Excerpt from Narrative Therapy with Dr. Bob Rich.

Website for Narrative Therapy: www.narrativeapproaches.com

Neurofeedback

Developed by: Hans Berger, G. Dietsch, Joe Kamiya, Elmer Green, Martin Orne, James Hardt, Barbara Brown, Barry Sterman, Joel Lubar, D.A. Quirk

Summary:

Neurofeedback is direct training of brain function, by which the brain learns to function more efficiently. We observe the brain in action from moment to moment. We show that information back to the person. And we reward the brain for changing its own activity to more appropriate patterns. This is a gradual learning process. It applies to any aspect of brain function that we can measure. Neurofeedback is also called EEG Biofeedback, because it is based on electrical brain activity, the electroencephalogram, or EEG. Neurofeedback is training in self-regulation. It is simply biofeedback applied to the brain directly.

Self-regulation is a necessary part of good brain function. Self-regulation training allows the system (the central nervous system) to function better.

Excerpt from EEG info

Neurofeedback (EEG Biofeedback) is a technique that enables a person to alter their brainwaves. It is used for many conditions and disabilities in which the brain is not working as well as it might. Neurofeedback helps control mood disorders like anxiety and depression, or problems with the central nervous system like conduct disorder, temper tantrums, specific learning disabilities or ADHD, sleep disorders, epilepsy, cognitive dysfunction resulting from head trauma, stroke, or aging. It is also used for patients undergoing cancer treatment, by reducing stress, pain and nausea, and enhancing immunity.

Excerpt from Neurofeedback Therapy

Website: http://www.neurofeedbacktherapy.net

Neuro-Linguistic Programming

Developed by: Richard Bandler & John Grinder

Summary:

Neuro Linguistic Psychotherapy (NLPt) is a specialised form of Neuro Linguistic Programming (NLP). The idea is that we work from and react to the world as we construct it from our experiences rather than directly from the "real world". We build our own unique models or maps of the world. Although all such maps are genuine to each of us, no one map is fully able to represent the "real world". Further, NLP is a way of exploring how people think, identifying success and then applying these successful actions or even beliefs in ways that work. This has proved practical and effective in a wide range of applications and situations. Using this form of what is called "modelling" change can be quite quick. NLPT is broadly based and draws on concepts from many areas of psychology and psychotherapy. Influences stem from the Gestalt 'school', the family therapy of Virginia Satir, Ericksonian brief therapy, and humanistic psychology. There are also clear links with the fields of systems theory, behavioural psychology and linguistics. More can be found on our web site. What happens in the therapy? The Neuro-Linguistic Psychotherapist and Counsellor will seek to help you, the client, to identify your desired states, i.e., your goals and dreams. You'll then seek to achieve them by using your own and new resources and skills. This can involve you in experimenting with changing beliefs that limit your success, identifying new beliefs, and/or gaining insights into patterns of your behaviour, which help you to have more choices.

Excerpt from Neuro Linguistic Psychotherapy and Counselling Association

Website Related to
Neuro-Linguistic Programming: www.nlptca.com, www.professionalguildofnlp.com

Psychodrama

Developed by: Jacob L. Moreno

Summary:

Psychodrama employs guided dramatic action to examine problems or issues raised by an individual. Using experiential methods, sociometry, role theory, and group dynamics, psychodrama facilitates insight, personal growth, and integration on cognitive, affective, and behavioral levels. It clarifies issues, increases physical and emotional well-being, enhances learning, and develops new skills. Psychodrama can be used in a group or individually for therapy and persona growth. It can also be applied to family and couples therapy.

Excerpt from British Psychodrama Association

Website Related to Psychodrama: http://gparrott.gotadsl.co.uk/BPA

SENSORIMOTOR PSYCHOLOGY

Developed by: Ron Kurtz

Summary:

Sensorimotor Psychotherapy is a method for facilitating the processing of unassimilated sensorimotor reactions to trauma and for resolving the destructive effects of these reactions on cognitive and emotional experience. These sensorimotor reactions consist of sequential physical and sensory patterns involving autonomic nervous system arousal and orienting/ defensive responses that seek to resolve to a point of rest and satisfaction in the body. During a traumatic event such a satisfactory resolution of responses might be accomplished by successfully fighting or fleeing. However, for the majority of traumatized clients, this does not occur. Traumatized individuals are plagued by the return of dissociated, incomplete or ineffective sensorimotor reactions in such forms as intrusive images, sounds, smells, body sensations, physical pain, constriction, numbing, and the inability to modulate arousal.

Excerpt from Traumatology

Sensorimotor Psychotherapy is a body-centered psychotherapy that makes it possible for clients to discover the habitual and automatic attitudes, both physical and psychological, by which they generate patterns of experience. This gentle therapy teaches clients to follow the inherently intelligent processes of body and mind to promote healing. It is particularly helpful in working with the effects of trauma and abuse, emotional pain, and limiting belief systems. Through the use of simple experiments, unconscious attitudes are brought to consciousness where they can be examined, understood, and changed.

Excerpt from Path out of Pain

Websites: www.sensorimotorpsychotherapy.org/index.html
www.fsu.edu/~trauma/v6i3/v6i3a3.html

SOMATIC EXPERIENCING

Developed by: Peter A. Levine, Ph.D.

Summary:

Somatic Experiencing® (SE) is a short-term naturalistic approach to the resolution and healing of trauma developed by Dr. Peter Levine. It is based upon the observation that wild prey animals, though threatened routinely, are rarely traumatized. Animals in the wild utilize innate mechanisms to regulate and discharge the high levels of energy arousal associated with defensive survival behaviors. These mechanisms provide animals with a built-in "immunity" to trauma that enables them to return to normal in the aftermath of highly "charged" life-threatening experiences. The theory postulates that the symptoms of trauma are the effect of a dysregulation of the autonomic nervous system (ANS). It further postulates that the ANS has an inherent capacity to self-regulate that is undermined by trauma, and that the inherent capacity to self-regulate can be restored by the procedures of

Somatic Experiencing. The procedure involves a client tracking his or her own felt-sense experience.

Excerpt from Foundation for Human Enrichment

Website: www.traumahealing.com

TRAUMA FOCUSED COGNITIVE BEHAVIORAL THERAPY

Developed by: J.A. Cohen, A.P. Mannarino, Knudsen, Staron

Summary:

Trauma-focused cognitive behavioral therapy (TF-CBT) is an evidence-based treatment approach shown to help children, adolescents, and their caretakers overcome trauma-related difficulties. It is designed to reduce negative emotional and behavioral responses following child sexual abuse and other traumatic events. The treatment—based on learning and cognitive theories—addresses distorted beliefs and an attribution related to the abuse and provides a supportive environment in which children are encouraged to talk about their traumatic experience. TF-CBT also helps parents who were not abusive to cope effectively with their own emotional distress and develop skills that support their children.

Excerpt from Child Welfare Information Gateway.

Trauma-Focused Cognitive-Behavioral Therapy (TF-CBT) is used for children and adolescents who have developed clinical levels of PTSD. In young children, this disorder is often the result of sexual or physical abuse. The program seeks to teach children skills to cope with the difficulties that this disorder creates. At the same time, therapy sessions are used to help children confront and deal with painful or scary past experiences.

Excerpt from Child Trends

Website: http://www.childtrends.org/lifecourse/programs/TraumaCBT.htm